Transference
Countertransference

Nathan Schwartz-Salant and Murray Stein, editors

Chiron Publications   •   Wilmette, Illinois

The Chiron Clinical Series
ISBN 0-933029-63-2

General Editors: Nathan Schwartz-Salant and Murray Stein
Managing Editor: Siobhan Drummond

Second Printing, 1993

© 1984, 1992 by Chiron Publications. All rights reserved. No part of this publication may be reproduced, stored in a retrieval system, or transmitted in any form, by any means, electronic, mechanical, photocopying, recording, or otherwise, without the prior written permission of the publisher, Chiron Publications, 400 Linden Avenue, Wilmette, Illinois 60091.

Printed in the United States of America

Book design by Elaine Hill.

Library of Congress Cataloging-in-Publication Data

Transference countertransference / Nathan Schwartz-Salant and Murray Stein, editors.
    p. cm. — (The Chiron clinical series)
    Originally published in the journal: Chiron : a review of Jungian analysis. c1984.
    Includes bibliographical references.
    ISBN 0-933029-63-2 : $15.95
    1. Transference (Psychology) 2. Countertransference (Psychology) I. Schwartz-Salant, Nathan, 1938- II. Stein, Murray, 1943- . III. Series.
    [DNLM: 1. Countertransference (Psychology) 2. Jungian Theory. 3. Physician-Patient Relations. 4. Transference (Psychology) WM 62 T772]
RC489.T73T72 1992
150.19'54—dc20
DNLM/DLC
for Library of Congress
        91-40546
        CIP

Contents

Archetypal Factors Underlying Sexual Acting-Out in the Transference/ Countertransference Process

Nathan Schwartz-Salant

Introduction

It is not difficult to recount the reasons that sexual acting-out in analysis is bad. There are in fact numerous contributions on this subject. Robert Stein's *Incest and Human Love* (1974, pp. 30–31) underscores the point that the imaginal faculty is damaged by incest wounds. Ann Ulanov's (1979) follow-up on the dreadful results of patient/analyst sex is an important contribution. Charles Taylor (1982) expresses a strong and apt ethical concern, stemming from an analysis of the danger to the soul that such behavior unleashes. Beverley Zabriskie (1982) probes the depths of wounding to women, and to the feminine in general, of such acts. Joseph Henderson (1982) provides a concise statement on the damage to the symbolic

Nathan Schwartz-Salant, Ph.D., University of California, Berkeley, and Diploma in Analytical Psychology, C. G. Jung Institute, Zurich, practices as a Jungian analyst in New York City, where he is on the faculty of the C. G. Jung Training Center. He is a past president of the National Association for the Advancement of Psychoanalysis (NAAP) and is the author of *Narcissism and Character Transformation: The Psychology of Narcissistic Character Disorders* (1982).

The footnotes in this paper are the result of the author's reflections on comments received at the 1983 Ghost Ranch Conference. He is grateful to the participants of the conference for their valuable remarks.

mode that sexual acting-out causes, emphasizing the same issue that Jung strongly identified in his major study, "The Psychology of the Transference" (1946, pars. 353–539). All these works explain in various ways the destructive—and here adjectives pile easily, but "destructive" will do—nature of the act. This listing does not exhaust Jungian contributions on the subject nor does it include the many non-Jungian criticisms of sex in analysis.

Sexual acting-out in the transference/countertransference process is one of the darkest shadows of the analytical endeavor. It is a shadow impulse against which all of the above contributions must be marshaled. But as Jungians we also know the importance of the integration of the shadow, not only of the need to repress it. In ethical mandates against sexual acting-out, which stem from an analysis of the carnage such behavior can wreak upon the soul, we gain structural attitudes that can be used in repression, and necessarily so. But the process of repression, while capable of drawing off the energy of this shadow impulse for conscious and symbolic use, also causes that shadow to take on its most vile, trickster-like qualities. If repression occurs rather than transformation, we engender a shadow side to analysis that works exactly as the shadow most commonly does: It gains the power to imperceptibly and insidiously dilute our best qualities and efforts. As we take refuge in moral and ethical restraint and appeal to the symbolic nature of analysis or reduce sexual acting-out to the abhorrent act of sex with the patient's infant Self (i.e., of sex with a child), we also set in motion a shadow that hardens our spirit, that casts our bodies as taboo and turns our sexuality into a symptom.

If I seem to stray a bit to the left, toward the sinister left-hand path, please understand that I am letting myself down into these depths so as to try to retrieve a bit of soul lost there and to understand more of the archetypal nature of the act. Otherwise, repression will end up being our method. I trust that it can be stated once and for all that sexual acting-out is not desirable and is generally destructive for all the reasons the fine papers I have mentioned enumerate.[1] But I want to know why it happens and why

---

1. The question can be raised as to whether my approach is itself repressive of archetypal powers. Is the "Goddess" offended at times by *not* acting-out sexually? Archetypal powers can be well served imaginally; furthermore, the acting-out of these energies can be, and usually is, a narcissistic inflation that deeply offends Her. The Goddess may be angry at not acting-out, but this is something that we can live with far better than her rage at acting-out in a space that cannot respect and serve Her. She can be revered in the sacred imaginal experience of the *coniunctio.*

it often seems to both analyst and analysand in the moment to be so true, in distinction to so false, an act. Is this merely a self-serving delusion, a Satanic trick of spiritual deceit? Or is it a kind of blundering after something elusive and hard to attain, a goal and purpose that have not been adequately addressed yet by Jung and Jungians? The latter is my belief. The elusive goal can be thought of as a substance that Jung called kinship libido and that I will refer to as *communitas,* following Victor Turner's (1974) analysis of liminal rites. This paper is about *communitas* and the central role the archetypal transference has in its release through the *coniunctio*— that image of the union of opposites that Jung found to be the structural form underlying the transference.

Jung's View of the Transference

Our understanding of the complexities of transference and countertransference dynamics becomes clearer as contributions about their underlying processes, rooted in early infant-mother conflicts, pour in from numerous clinicians with various points of view. We have come a long way since Breuer fled from his patient's sexual fantasies; we have come through a period when the counter-transference was thought to be a regrettable failing and into a new domain, in more recent years, where we are becoming more comfortable with the transference/countertransference process as a mode of transferring information. An analyst's reactions are now, in many quarters, looked to for objective information about the patient, and the patient's communications and dreams are recognized as indicating accurate perceptions of the analyst and the state of the analytical process. To begin even to mention references in the literature to the above statements would throw open the door to many more citations of extremely valuable clinical work. Our knowledge seems to be mounting, and bridges are more easily crossed between different schools of thought. The existence of archetypal elements in the transference is now less obscure, and as Kleinian contributions are assimilated by the psychoanalytic community, we can imagine closer ties forming between Jungian and non-Jungian approaches, links that have been pioneered by the London School of Analytical Psychology. Such bridges seem ready-made, since object relations theory stresses the purposeful or goal-oriented nature of the psyche, a mainstay of the Jungian approach.

Differences too can be cited, and conflict among the various schools of thought also grows. The roles of envy, rage, fear, object loss, drives, goals, spirit, instinct, fantasy, and idealization, constitute an arena for a discussion that is the obverse of the one I just sketched out. Rather than harmony, I could have stressed conflicting points of view, but this, too, only underscores the advance in our knowledge. We seem to know a lot, at least much more than we did nearly 40 years ago when Jung wrote "The Psychology of the Transference."

The question arises, then, as to the value of the strange, alchemically oriented approach Jung employed in this work, his major statement on the transference. Have we outgrown it? Should we consider it in the same way Jung viewed alchemy, as groping in the dark in lieu of better understanding? Is it largely of historical interest, an example of emerging consciousness, and, like alchemical speculations, something of great, albeit obscure, value from which we must now extract consciousness with our greatly expanded knowledge of the transference/countertransference process?

This paper is not primarily an account of Jung's view of the transference. My concern is with a more narrow topic, the issue of sexual acting-out in the transference/countertransference process. But the way to understand this lies, I think, precisely in re-thinking the imagery of the alchemical text, the *Rosarium Philosophorum*. Jung took this text as a guide because, as he said, "Everything that the doctor discovers and experiences when analysing the unconscious of his patient coincides in the most remarkable way with the content of these pictures" (1946, par. 401). By further exploring the symbolism of the *coniunctio*—that image of the union of opposites that Jung found to be the structural form underlying the transference—and its possible existence as an imaginal *experience* in the here and now, we can better understand sexual acting-out in analysis. This requires both that we build upon Jung's analysis and that we also depart from some of his conclusions.

"The Psychology of the Transference," we should not forget, was an offshoot of Jung's great opus, *Mysterium Coniunctionis* (see Hannah 1976, p. 198). That work hardly mentions the word transference, but its subtitle, *An Inquiry into the Separation and Synthesis of Psychic Opposites in Alchemy,* shows it to be implicitly concerned with the transference. Jung understood transference as a process in which opposites, such as the analyst's anima and the analysand's animus, need to be separated, taken out of a state of *participation mystique,* and then integrated into ego-consciousness to partake ultimately in the formation in consciousness of an individual, symbolic sense of the Self.

My approach differs from Jung's in two ways. First, the *coniunctio* is, in my view, to be understood not only as an unconscious ordering factor, part of an archetypal process which, as Jung says, "as a rule . . . passes off in a series of dreams and is discovered only retrospectively, when the dream material comes to be analysed" (1946, par. 461). It is also to be seen as an imaginal experience between two people in the here and now. Clinical material will clarify this. Experienced in the present, the *coniunctio* yields that mysterious quality, kinship, which Jung finds to be at the root of the transference. The *coniunctio* yields kinship in a more intense, integrated, and transforming manner when actually experienced consciously and recognized for what it is than when it is part of an unconscious process and hardly noticed in the here and now. It is a blundering and compulsive search for this substance, kinship or *communitas,* which underlies much of sexual acting-out in analysis.

Second, the goal of the alchemical process as depicted in the *Rosarium Philosophorum* is the hermaphrodite. Jung finds this untenable as an end product. I differ on this evaluation. It is not only *communitas* that emerges in the transference/countertransference process, but a new and viable hermaphroditic Self image.

In "The Psychology of the Transference," Jung considers the image of the hermaphrodite, known as the Rebis, to be a regrettable product of the alchemist's undeveloped consciousness. He accounts for this by citing the alchemist's lack of awareness of the fundamental psychological process of projection, and he sees this image as deriving from the "immaturity of the alchemist's mind" and the alchemist's lack of psychological understanding (1946, par. 533). Consequently, "nature could say no more than that the combination of supreme opposites was a hybrid thing. And there the statement stuck, in sexuality, as always when the potentialities of consciousness do not come to the assistance of nature" (1946, par. 533). He continues his assault on the image of the Rebis by noting that things remained in this condition until

> at the end of the nineteenth century, Freud dug up this problem again. . . . The sexuality of the unconscious was instantly taken up with great seriousness and elevated to a sort of religious dogma. . . . The sexualism of the hermaphrodite symbol completely overpowered consciousness and gave rise to an attitude of mind which is just as

unsavoury as the old hybrid symbolism. . . . The sexualism of these
contents always denotes an unconscious identity of the ego with an
unconscious figure . . . and because of this the ego is obliged, willing
and reluctant at once, to be a party to the hierosgamos, or at least to
believe that it is simply and solely a matter of erotic consummation.
And sure enough it increasingly becomes so the more one . . . concen-
trates on the sexual aspect and the less attention one pays to the
archetypal patterns. . . . I have never come across the hermaphrodite as
a personification of the goal, but more a symbol of the initial state,
expressing an identity with anima or animus. (1946, pars. 533–35)

"The Psychology of the Transference," centering as it does
upon the alchemical goal of the Rebis, is a strong injunction
against sexual acting-out in analysis. One must wonder if this
problematic shadow aspect of analysis was responsible for Jung's
negative view of the Rebis. And was his intense aversion to Freud's
view of sexuality a contributing factor? For it is, as far as I know,
only in his work on the transference that the Rebis is seen as
negative. In *Mysterium Coniunctionis*, the Rebis is always mentioned without negative judgment; indeed, it is praised. There it is
noted as an image for the paradoxical union of opposites, of
sulphur and the "radical moisture," which are, as Jung says, "the
two most potent opposites imaginable" (1955, par. 337). Jung
quotes Dorn: "It has within it both corruption and preservation
against corruption, for in the natural order there is nothing that
does not contain as much evil as good" (1955, par. 337). Jung
understands the alchemical symbol of the peacock's tail—an image of the integration of all psychic qualities—as representing the
unity of the Rebis. And in "The Psychology of the Child Archetype," the Rebis is seen not "as a product of primitive non-differ-
entiation. . . . On the contrary, man's imagination has been preoc-
cupied with this idea over and over again on the high and even
the highest levels of culture" (1949, par. 292). Only in "The
Psychology of the Transference" is the Rebis seen in a negative
light. It is likely that Jung regarded both the danger of sexual
acting-out and the tendency to reduce the psyche to derivations of
the sexual instinct, as he understood Freud's aim to be, as factors
requiring him totally to side against the image of the hermaphrodite. "The Psychology of the Transference" is concerned with the
dangers of this image. As a natural goal, it must be countered by
consciousness and understanding of projections. The entire work
is filled with ethical concerns and moralistic interpretations of a
sort not found in Jung's other works. Fordham (1974, p. 18) has

aptly criticized Jung's frequent recourse to morals in "The Psychology of the Transference," a point of view with which I agree.

There is no doubt that the hermaphrodite can be a negative image, often found at the beginning of an analytic process. For example, the hermaphrodite may be an image for the kind of union that forms between analyst and patient in a process dominated by splitting and projective identification. The two people can easily feel glued together in one affective body, partaking of the same emotions, while each maintains different defenses and attitudes: one body, two heads! Also, the hermaphroditic Self can be seen ruling the analyst's tendency to act as if we were whole, while our "wholeness" is actually a hybrid thing, made up partly of the patient's introjects: We are two, thinking we are one. In this confused mixture, we easily tend to make partial interpretations and mistake them to be whole. We tell a patient about dynamics and are surprised to find out this was devastating, for we failed to note how it was only a part of the ego we were describing. We assume, all too easily, that the patient has access to those other parts, yet they are split off and unavailable. Such psychological states can dominate the transference/countertransference process: The Self we feel is often a hybrid object of parts of us stuck together with parts of the patient. And the patient is also easily ruled by a similar hybrid state.

I have been describing the hybrid nature of a Self structure that can be mutually dominant in analysis through *participation mystique*. The hermaphrodite is also a fitting image for the Self structure in persons suffering from narcissistic and borderline personality disorders. The latter are especially known for their splitting mechanisms, in which mutually exclusive states exist side by side without affecting one another. Or they affect each other totally: A male patient feels hatred toward me and then immediately shifts to loving statements, without losing a beat; a woman feels sexual toward me if she feels young, but completely asexual if she feels her age. The two states exist simultaneously, both defining identity, and together they are extremely confusing—for both of us. Each opposite seems both to deplete and excite the other. Gender identity is also confused. The Self is hermaphroditic.

Amidst the chaotic and despairing feelings such a Self image creates, the tendency to act-out sexually is heightened. For sexuality seems to hold out the remarkable promise to unify the opposites into a meaningful, harmonious whole and to transform their hybrid, monstrous state. There is little doubt that the hermaphrodite can show its highly dangerous quality most centrally in relationships, easily tricking us into believing that sexual acts (or compulsive interpretations) are acts of the True Self and are healing as well.

The negative aspect of the hermaphrodite is the dominant shadow of analysis, and sexual acting-out is one of its more dangerous behavior patterns. But, as Jung's other work shows, the hermaphrodite is not only negative; in fact, it can be a highly positive image. Only by understanding this, I believe, will we be able to see the other side of sexual acting-out: not a "good side," but an aspect that offers a meaningful context to this behavior.

Sexual acting-out can be interpreted in many ways. It can be regarded through the lens of the analyst's own childhood neuroses, especially those which derive from oedipal wounds caused by parental rejection of sexuality. It is also commonly interpreted as an attempt to integrate split-off, schizoid sectors of the psyche, sectors in which oedipal and pre-oedipal sexuality—the latter containing archetypal or impersonal sexual energies—are contained along with intense frustrations and despair. All of this is dangerously released through the negative archetypal aspect of the Rebis. But our understanding of sexual acting-out approaches completeness, and opens up to an understanding that can lead to transformation rather than to repression, only when we appreciate the positive nature of the Rebis.

As the *Rosarium* texts show, the archetypal process underpinning the transference/countertransference process can create a hermaphroditic Self. That is, the individuation process, when experienced not primarily as a solitary work of introversion but as a coupled process with another person, can create a hermaphroditic Self structure. This is quite different from other descriptions of the goal, such as the circle, square, mandala, and the superior personality, which Jung much prefers in "The Psychology of the Transference" (1946, par. 535). These latter images best describe an individual Self, but the hermaphrodite, on the other hand, can be not only an individual image but also a conjoined Self. The Rebis represents a psychic reality that can stem from two people's achieving the *coniunctio* as an imaginal act. This reality is seen through the imagination that we bring to this remarkable linking of souls, the *coniunctio*, and through the imagination born of this same union. The central issue is that, contrary to the spirit where the individual Self is regarded as the pearl of great price, a Self can be created between, and of, two people without a negative *participation mys-*

tique dominating and without either person losing identity. With proper use of imagination and integrated experience of sexuality as an energy field, two people can experience the Self and return to this Self again and again, just as an individual does when the Self is felt as a consolidated center of the personality. The same uplifting spirit, order, wisdom, and gnosis can be gained from this Self.

There are also significant differences between the two experiences of the Self. We can begin to understand what these differences are by reflecting on "The New Birth" in the *Rosarium Philosophorum* (see fig. 1), in which the Rebis is born and is pictured standing on the moon. This image refers to the domain of psychic reality that Jung called the somatic unconscious, or the subtle body, in his seminars on Nietzsche's *Thus Spake Zarathustra* (1934, Pt. 1, Lecture 4; cf. Schwartz-Salant 1982, pp. 119–20, for a further commen-

Figure 1. The New Birth. (This appears as Figure 10 in the *Rosarium Philosophorum;* see Jung 1946, p. 307.)

tary). From Jung's analysis we are led to conclude that it also refers to a synchronistic experience, of which the *coniunctio* is a prime example. The experience of *coniunctio* between two people is an act of "grace," and yet the imaginal product of this experience, the image of a conjoined, hermaphroditic Self perceived in the space between them, can be returned to from time to time. It appears we can increase the probability of its recurrence through correct technique, and yet we are always still dealing with synchronistic phenomena, not with ego-determined events. That speaks to one of the blunders of sexual acting-out: It is a poor variant on sexual magic in a setting that can least tolerate it.

The hermaphrodite and the image of the conjoined Self will occupy us throughout the rest of this paper. Now, however, we can consider the other issue on which I find myself at odds with Jung's approach. The *coniunctio*, as experienced between two people, leads to the release of a special kind of energy or "substance," called kinship libido, which is the essence of the transference:

> Kinship libido—which could still engender a satisfying feeling of belonging together, as for instance in the early Christian communities—has long been deprived of its object. But, being an instinct, it is not to be satisfied by any mere substitute such as a creed, party, nation, or state. It wants the *human* connection. That is the core of the whole transference phenomenon. (Jung 1946, par. 445)

It is an unconscious, hence also a compulsive, search for the precious substance of *communitas* that plays a central role in sexual acting-out in analysis. Without underestimating the motivations stemming from an analyst's and an analysand's repressed infantile sexuality, there is this other aim that accounts for the abandon, the irresponsibility, the risk taking, and often the strange sense of being true to one's Self in sexual acting-out. This is the kinship libido or *communitas*, and this can be released by the imaginally experienced *coniunctio*, which is foolishly sought in concrete sexual acts. The central point I want to make in what follows is that this precious substance, as well as the Self structure between two people that accompanies its release, cannot adequately be understood as the result of a largely unconscious process, analogous to that between mother and child, or simply as the archetypal underside of an adult relationship. Furthermore, again in contrast with Jung's structural emphasis, the kinship libido released from the imaginally experienced *coniunctio* is different from what is achieved by the integration of projections in the transference/countertransference process.

The Self that is born as an inner psychic reality neither satisfies the wish for nor creates the experience of *communitas* that underlies the transference/countertransference. It is the mutually and imaginally experienced *coniunctio* that helps us grasp the dynamics of *communitas* and the archetypal aspects underlying sexual acting-out in the transference/countertransference.

The Nature of the *Coniunctio* Experience: Liminality

A central result of the *coniunctio* experience is an I-Thou relationship. This brings a sense of mutual respect, equality, and concern on a very deep level, as if blood had been exchanged. The term often used for this experience is *communitas*. *Communitas* implies not only the structure of communion or community but also a kind of "substance," as though it could be transmitted; it is neither a purely physical nor a purely psychic reality but a paradoxical combination of them.

These are metaphors for experience and not mere abstractions or conceptions. These metaphors attempt to capture experiences that happen in a realm that is felt to be outside a normal time sense and in a space felt to have substance. This space, long known as the subtle body, exists because of imagination, yet it also has autonomy. The *coniunctio* occurs in it. The archetypal processes of which it partakes are depicted in the *Rosarium Philosophorum*. Events in this space, like those in the atom, have their own archetypal laws, but when people engage them, with and through their imagination, they will often apprehend different imagery of the *coniunctio*. These images, while not identical, generally complement one another. In Jung's discussion of the imagination in *Psychology and Alchemy* (1953, par. 360; see also pars. 390–96), these images derive from true imagination, in distinction to fantastic imagination. The experience of *communitas*, which is released through the *coniunctio*, will be neither personal nor archetypal but an inseparable mixture of both.

For purposes of understanding the archetypal background of sexual acting-out in the transference/countertransference process, we must look especially to the nature of the transitional realm in which the *coniunctio* occurs. This is a liminal state.

The term "liminal" is borrowed from van Gennep's study of rites of passage (cf. Turner 1974, pp. 131ff.). It denotes the middle phase of rites of passage, which is preceded by rites of separation (from an earlier state) and is followed by rites of reincorporation (toward a new status that has integrated the results of the liminal experience). The integratable nature of liminal experience is of the essence. By way of contrast, a good deal of hallucinogenic drug use leads into liminality but very rarely results in any structural changes of a positive nature. Instead, it is usually a kind of bath in anti-structure. The products of liminality experienced in rites of passage and in the *coniunctio* experience, however, carry over into the post-liminal period.

Turner (1974) describes the liminal state as follows: "During the liminal period, the state of the ritual subject ... becomes ambiguous, neither here nor there, betwixt all fixed points of classification; he passes through a symbolic domain that has few or none of the attributes of his past or coming state. . . . It is in liminality that *communitas* emerges" (p. 232). Turner (1974, p. 286) quotes a lovely poem, which captures the liminal state:

> If they see
> breasts and long hair coming
> they call it woman,
> if beard and whiskers
> they call it man;
> but, look, the self that hovers
> in between
> is neither man
> nor woman
> O Rāmanātha.

The experience of the *coniunctio* is often one in which one feels neither male nor female, and the "self that hovers/in between" can be hermaphroditic.[2]

Turner's account also tells of the energies and structures that can be released in liminal experience:

---

2. The "self that hovers/in between" is an imaginal creation. What is involved here is a kind of vision or "seeing" similar to active imagination, but it is imagination that flares or rises up. In the visions at Eleusis, the initiates identified with Demeter, who can partially be understood as the somatic unconscious (Schwartz-Salant 1982, pp. 149–50). It is a particular state of being in the body through which imagination arises. As in the Eleusinian Rites, which were preceded by the Lesser Mysteries of a Dionysian nature, this imaginal state is nurtured by the preceding interactions, which include intense, erotic energies akin to those depicted in "The King and Queen" in the *Rosarium* (see fig. 5). These are preliminary to the *coniunctio*. The *coniunctio* is always an act of grace, a synchronistic occurrence, which can never be forced. It would be a great misapprehension of my meaning to understand anything in this paper as sexual seduction or as sexual magic.

In many mythologies, the gods slay or unman their fathers, mate with their mother and sisters, copulate with mortals in the form of animals and birds—while in rites that act these out, their human representatives or imitators imitate, in symbol or sometimes even literally, these immortal amoralities. . . . [There] may even be episodes of real or symbolic cannibalism. . . . [In liminal rites] there are regularities and repetitions [that are] not yet those of law and custom but of unconscious cravings which stand opposed to the norms in which social bonding secularly depends—to the rules of exogamy and the prohibition of incest. . . . [In liminal rites there are] certain key symbols and central symbolic actions [that are] "culturally intended" to arouse a gross quantum of affect—even of illicit affect—only to attach this quantum of affect divested of moral qualities, in a later phase of a great ritual to licit and legitimate goals and values. (1974, p. 257)

The liminal state is one where "in symbol or sometimes even literally" the rules of exogamy and incest can be broken, so that the energies of "unconscious cravings" are released. Through such "immortal amoralities" a "gross quantum of affect," not otherwise accessible, is released. It is the blundering, compulsive, and highly unconscious search for these energies that is always a part of sexual acting-out in analysis. In primitive rites, there is always a careful control by the "elders" and an awareness that the liminal state must be entered and left with care, so that the experience will not be destructive but can be integrated back into time-space existence.

The *Rosarium Philosophorum* also depicts a necessary "control," but here it is an archetypal power, the descending dove representing the Holy Ghost (Jung 1946, par. 419). This is the image of the results of the *coniunctio* as an *unio mystica*, the soul's union with the transcendent Godhead, which then forms a vertical counterbalance to the energies released in the tantric-like unions represented by the alchemist and *soror mystica*. The Holy Ghost can also, of course, represent ecclesiastical wisdom. As Jung notes, we should recognize that some kind of control is necessary. In the *Rosarium* it derives from the spirit archetype. In the early stages of forming the *coniunctio*, Eros alone is not sufficient. This point is extremely important. It coincides with my experience that the *coniunctio* is both spiritual and sexual, and its fruitful existence fades or leads to disaster when either of these aspects is missing. Concerning the role of the spirit archetype, it is doubtful that ethical codes and concern for the analytical frame can take its place. These may prevent the occurrence of sexual acting-out in analysis, but they can also block the occurrence of the imaginal experience of the *coniunctio*. "One law for the Lion and Ox is Oppression," says Blake (cited in Turner 1974, p. 286), referring to such moral tyranny.

Clinical Example

I have been seeing Mary for four years. It was several years before I recognized her deep spiritual connection. This had been largely a private matter between her ego and a schizoid sector of her personality. During the sessions, I would spend much time splitting in a way brought about by her own splitting process and my counter-transference. I consistently noted this behavior, and gradually she and I began, so to speak, to be in the room. Considerable effort was also made to analyze a secret inflation. This was not identical with her authentic spiritual connection but rather consisted of a power fantasy in which she was the Prime Minister. This schizoid material was well concealed by her persona and splitting defenses. She functioned well professionally but complained of poor relationships and insufficient professional acclaim. Several months prior to the sessions I will describe, she could express what she felt to be very negative feelings and could vent them, as she said, "without any concern for your feelings. I don't give a damn!" She had never said such a thing to anyone before. I experienced her seeming attack as a relief because now she was more present than ever before. I had experienced her splitting and withdrawal as a torment, and they had often aroused my anger.

The following are brief recollections of the session preceding the one in which the *coniunctio* was experienced. I felt a lack of interest in her, I was rather bored, and I easily tended to lose focus and to dissociate. I told her this and she recognized that she too was splitting.[3] It was hard for me to be present, and she could under-

---

3. The description of these sessions readily raises many questions. It is easy to regard the patient's splitting as induced by my countertransference. It is also possible to take the transformation of the sadistic brother image (discussed later) as simply a transference statement, representing the patient's response to my not attacking her with interpretations of her splitting. It is also natural to ask about boundaries: Is all the dissociation simply a result of too loose boundaries on my part, or a fear of intrusion in the patient? Or is it caused by a fear that I have poor boundaries and hence that the analytical container is unsafe? Questions such as these were raised when I presented this paper at the Ghost Ranch Conference. I was also quite aware of them in working through the clinical material. The approach of Goodheart (see pp. 89–117 in this issue), who has incorporated Robert Langs's method, could be

stand how this fit her expectations, but only partially. She said it was also my problem, for at times she felt she did not have this expectancy, particularly at the beginning of the hour when I experienced the greatest difficulty in being present. We tried to sort this out. I felt resistant; so did she.

In the next session, she began by saying that she had been angry all week since last seeing me. She restated her view that in the last session she had not expected rejection and that I was splitting from her and was uninterested in her. In contrast to the last session, she was now unusually present.

Mary then spoke about her brother, who, she said, "always put me down, always humiliated me." I felt a new kind of clarity; I intuitively understood how her ego split. There is a union between one part of her ego and the spirit; the two of them are in a distant connection, far from the here and now. Then there is another union, also split off, between another part of her ego and her brother, who represents an inner persecuting force. I made this interpretation, and she found that it made sense. She went on to say the following: "He tells me I am uninteresting, and I align with him and give up on anyone liking me. I also become uninterested in communicating with you." I reflected that last time I was filled with the introject of her brother, and I also reacted neurotically to her resistance to communicating with me. I reacted by being withdrawn, matching what I experienced as her withdrawal from me. As we discussed these projections she recalled that when she was angry months ago, it felt good not to have to care about my feelings. I told her that when she is angry I feel she is present. "Last time," she said, "I

---

focused upon my method with interesting results. However, we are dealing here with fundamental issues that I can only allude to in this note, issues that speak directly to the subject of psychological healing. Jung wrote that the *numinosum* (1973, pp. 376–77) is the healing agent in therapy. A good deal of acumen can go into observing the clinical interaction, with special attention to the destructive effects of the analyst's splitting. But this kind of approach, while of importance, can also have the negative effect of seeing everything that transpires in the patient and between analyst and patient as a direct result of some intervention, some interpretation, or some behavior of the analyst. It overlooks the healing force of nontransferential, archetypal factors. It focuses our attention in a manner that is not attuned to the symbolic and numinuous products of the psyche. As the latter, especially in the synchronistic occurrence of the *coniunctio,* are a rare occurrence, they are even more readily overlooked or blocked. Thus, while I can reflect upon my behavior in this case and recognize that the patient may have been adversely affected by me in ways I was unaware of, I still strongly favor the approach I took because it is attuned to the numinous and does not neglect the healing factor in favor of a microscopic analysis of the analytical interaction.

experienced you as a kind of judge, a Hades type of judge." She explained that when she inwardly begins to feel young and has the experience of her inner child, I am critical of this child, especially when she presents problems with relationships. I thought that I understood the Hades metaphor, for I frequently feel an inner rising-up of energies that want to penetrate her, to "shove an interpretation down her throat."

We continued in this way, trying to sort out projections and reality. Then, in a spontaneous insight, I became aware that another element dominates her relationship with her brother: There is an incest link. I told her this intuition and she said she could feel sexuality toward her brother. This was a new experience. She then mentioned a man she disliked and noted that there was no sexuality in him, just detached sadism. I took this as a special enjoinder not to withdraw.

At this point something unusual happened. As I was aware of the incestuous link she had with her brother, I experienced an erotic energy field between us. She also experienced it. As we both felt this energy, which seemed like something between us, my consciousness lowered a bit and, just as in active imagination, I saw a shimmering image, which partook of both of us, move upwards from where it was, near the ground. I told her this. She said, "Yes, I also see it, but I'm afraid of it." I continued to share what I saw and experienced. I saw the image between us as white; she saw a kind of fluid that had a center. She said she knew that if she descended into her body, it would be too intense, that she was afraid. She stated that she now felt I was her friend, that it felt like an I-Thou relationship, and that she had never had such an experience before with anyone. She told me that she was afraid and felt herself slipping away. I responded that she needed only to embody more, only to come down into her body. A feeling of timelessness pervaded; I didn't know if one minute or twenty had passed. She worried about next time. What would she do if this experience weren't there again? She said she felt that I was extremely powerful and sensual, but for the first time this didn't frighten her because she also felt equality. A sense of kinship, a brother-sister feeling, was clear to both of us. And there *was* a pull toward sexual enactment, toward physical union, but this tendency had its own inhibition, as if the energy field between us oscillated, separating and joining us in a kind of sine wave rhythm. This was clearest when we allowed our imagination to *see* the other. Withdrawal of *seeing* tends to obscure awareness of the dynamics and the inhibitions within the experience. Mary recognized this experience as a *coniunctio* and also commented that it was happening in the subtle body. This awareness is typical of the "gnosis-yielding" nature of the *coniunctio* experience.

The hour came to a close. The kinship feeling that was released by this union was potent. Not only did it bring us closer in a way that felt like kin, like blood relationship, but it resulted in a remarkable transformation in Mary's inner life. In the next session, she told of a dream in which, for the first time she could recall, her brother was a positive figure, helping her learn a subject with which she had always had difficulty. I have seen this kind of result many times: After the *coniunctio* experience, there is a transformation of inner sadistic anima or animus figures.

The Archetypal Transference/Countertransference

The *coniunctio* experience corresponds to "The Conjunction" in the *Rosarium Philosophorum* (see fig. 2). In the sessions that followed this experience with Mary, a depression occurred, depicted by "Death" in the *Rosarium* (see fig. 3). This seems always to be

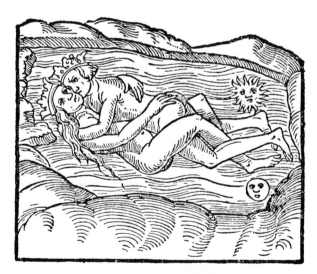

Figure 2. The Conjunction. (This appears as Figure 5 in the *Rosarium Philosophorum;* see Jung 1946, p. 249.)

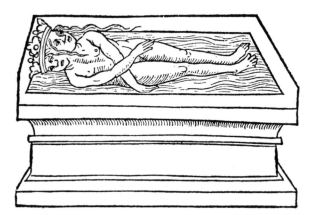

Figure 3. Death. (This appears as Figure 6 in the
Rosarium Philosophorum; see Jung 1946, p. 259.)

the case after the *coniunctio*. But the depression, or *nigredo* state, that occurs is not a regression to earlier stages of analysis; rather, a sense of purpose or finality in the process initiated by the *coniunctio* persists. Here amplification, as Jung describes it, is quite to the point (1946, par. 478). For example, Mary was depressed several sessions later. She told of an awful experience she had had with an uncle. For introverts especially, depression is often initiated at this time by an outer event. In the past we would have had to work on this experience or on its relationship to the transference. Now it was necessary to remember what had transpired and to amplify the archetypal nature of the process, with reference here to Jung's study of the imagery in the *Rosarium*. The depression quickly lifted. Also, as in "The Ascent of the Soul" in the *Rosarium* (see fig. 4), which Jung describes as a state of "soul loss" (1946, par. 477), a lack of connection existed in the next session. With Mary this lack of connection was mild; it was a kind of deadness that strongly contrasted with the *coniunctio* experience. In other cases, I have witnessed the ushering in of intense processes, even psychotic transferences. Early seductions, rape experiences, or dangers felt from the parental unconscious, and especially experiences of the patient's Dionysian-like energies being rejected at a young age, all clamor for attention at this stage. Strong negative transferences can emerge; sometimes they quickly pass, at other times not so quickly.

In total contradiction to expectations that the *coniunctio* experience might be a kind of collusion or seduction that sidesteps the

Figure 4. The Ascent of the Soul. (This appears as
Figure 7 in the *Rosarium Philosophorum;* see Jung
1946, p. 269.)

negative transference, the most intense negative transferences frequently emerge after it. It seems that the *coniunctio* and the released sense of deep kinship form a kind of archetypal representation of what is known as the therapeutic alliance, but the trust
released by the *coniunctio* is far deeper than that alliance. With
greater trust and containment stemming from the *coniunctio*, it
appears that more can be risked—for example, aspects of psyche
that have little containment (i.e., parts in which there is no operative
Self, or Self feeling). These can now enter analysis and be worked
through.

The *coniunctio* is an unusual and remarkable experience. It is
by far the exception to what ordinarily occurs in an analytical
process, yet it does exist. When it occurs, it heals very old wounds.
Incest wounds especially need to be mentioned, as well as those
excruciating psychic attacks a child may feel when sexuality emerges.

Such traumas feel like attacks by God. Attacks upon incestuous fantasies and acts in childhood, while generally incurred through some personal intervention of a parent or a betrayal, are often felt as impersonal and require an archetypal as well as a personal cure.

The fact that the *coniunctio* can happen in the here and now, with healing results, accounts for the motive behind a good deal of sexual acting-out. This behavior can be seen as a kind of forced sexual magic stemming from split-off parts of the analyst's and analysand's psyche, which are mingled with archetypal factors. If the *coniunctio* could not happen, and if it did not lead to healing, I doubt that sexual acting-out would occur and be so much of a problem.

While incestuous energy—psyche's endogamous tendency, as Jung called it—does not dominate the *coniunctio*, it is part of the medium. The energy of incest, which is a Dionysian-like affect that was never properly received in childhood, is now experienced with a "brother" or "sister" to the higher goal of creating kinship. In a sense "the complex cures the complex." Incestuous energy, perhaps better called Dionysian energy, gains a proper container in the analytic *coniunctio*. In a sense, incest is committed on the level of the subtle body; it is not sublimated into things spiritual nor is it repressed, and this is why the *coniunctio* often has an embarrassing quality. But incestuous issues, stemming from a child's Dionysian past, are only part of the larger reality of the *coniunctio* experience. This experience has a wide-ranging transformative effect. I have already mentioned the change that can occur in what were once sadistic inner figures. Another potential of the *coniunctio* experience is the birth of the ego. When this experience occurs in a person with a false Self personality structure, for example, in someone with borderline features, it can have the effect of aiding the birth, or what Fordham (1957, p. 117) would call the deintegration, of the ego.

One further note about incest energies. If they are not available because of severe oedipal repressions or because of the dominance of pre-oedipal defences that are controlled by splitting mechanisms, there is less likelihood of the occurrence of the *coniunctio*. These incestuous energies are portrayed in "King and Queen" in the *Rosarium* (Jung 1946, pars. 410–49) (see fig. 5). This is not the image of the *coniunctio*, which occurs in "The Conjunction" (see fig. 2), but unless the incestuous energies of what Jung calls the "left-hand path" are available to consciousness, the archetypal transference will only partially reach its potential and will rarely lead to

Figure 5. King and Queen. (This appears as Figure 2 in the *Rosarium Philosophorum;* see Jung 1946, p. 213.)

the *coniunctio* with another person. The necessity for incest libido to be part of the transformation process leading to the *coniunctio* is an important factor in sexual acting-out, which can be an unconscious attempt to add to these energies. Aside from the destructive effects that generally follow, it is poor alchemy.

The *coniunctio* can form in many ways, and each instance is significantly different. Sometimes the picture in the *Rosarium* that follows the actual *coniunctio* and that shows both lovers having wings (see fig. 6) is paradigmatic. This represents an experience in which each person feels a lifting sensation. As they continue to be channels for spiritual and erotic energies, which tend to intensify as each imaginally *sees* the other more deeply, the *coniunctio* between them is felt to rise, and they too feel a lifting sensation.

The *coniunctio* can also be experienced without a direct, face-to-face encounter. Two people may experience a kind of current

Figure 6. The Conjunction. (This appears as Figure
5a in the *Rosarium Philosophorum;* see Jung 1946, p.
251.)

flowing between them, a flow with more than erotic quality, even
during a telephone hour. In one such instance, a patient was
reporting a numinous dream with tantric-like imagery. She dreamed
of an androgynous young man who reached an orgasm that sprayed
a golden fluid over her, yet it also traveled in a circle that seemed to
be self-renewing. While the dream was being recounted, a *coniunctio* could be felt between us, with the kind of sharing of imaginal
experiences "occurring in the space between," as in Mary's case.
This *coniunctio* was a very different union from the transference/
countertransference bond that had dominated our work for months
and that had found special focus in her personal oedipal complex
activated in the transference. Now there was a qualitative difference
stemming from an archetypal element. As usual, this was followed
by a *nigredo* state, a seemingly inexplicable fall into depression.
After a *coniunctio* experience, this depression is composed of
previously unintegrated, or only partially dealt with, personal complexes. In this case they were hostile qualities rooted in her father's

lack of response to her sexuality, and a belief that I would behave in the same way. Reductive analysis was not called for at this time, however. A process with its own goal had been strongly constellated, and recollection of the *coniunctio* experience and amplification of it with reference to the *Rosarium* imagery was sufficient to contain the depression and regain a sense of connection between us. Within this process, the patient could readily accept the personal shadow material that was the content of her depression, and the depression then lifted.

The stage in the *Rosarium* known as the "Ascent of the Soul" (see fig. 4) followed, as it did in Mary's case. There was a feeling of deadness between us during the next telephone hour. This also carried previously unintegrated, pre-oedipal elements of a narcissistic nature. But, once again, reference to the process occurring between us in the here and now was the essential task, not reductive analysis. It appears that the analyst's role at this stage is largely one of remembering, a task often made difficult by depressive affects and projective identification. I would also note that at times it is the analyst's countertransference, and not the patient's transference, that reflects the "soul loss" Jung speaks of. At times a patient will return after a *coniunctio* experience and be very present and engaged, whereas the analyst tends to be withdrawn, his soul not in the encounter. Such behavior can be extremely painful for the patient. As a result of the *coniunctio*, however, individuals often stand up for themselves and point out the analyst's problem in ways previously unavailable to the ego.

I have included this reference to the analyst's countertransference carrying the "soul-loss" experience because it is an important clinical factor. In the case that was carried out by telephone, this was not an issue. I remembered the *coniunctio* and reminded her of it; with that the deadness lifted and narcissistic issues, especially preoccupation with appearance, could be readily integrated.

I have emphasized the importance of the availability of sexual energies for the *coniunctio* experience. I have done this because the *coniunctio* I am speaking of occurs with another person, and in that form sexuality is extremely important. But of equal importance is the spirit. Every instance of the *coniunctio* that I have experienced with another person has occurred with someone for whom spiritual awareness was central to life's meaning. I will not discuss this in detail here because my main emphasis is on sexual acting-out; hence I am concentrating on sexuality in the *coniunctio*. But this focus is one-sided. The *coniunctio* experience is both spiritual and sexual, and it synthesizes these opposites. I apologize for this one-sidedness, which may especially be felt by women, for whom, as Jung (1961, p. 387) says, sexuality is far more spiritual than for men, for whom it is more earthly an instinct.

Liminality and Jung's Approach to the Transference

Jung appealed strongly to ethics and morality in his analysis of the transference, but most central to his approach is the absolute necessity of treating the intense energy transfer and structural changes of the transference as projections. His model for dealing with what he refers to as the endogamous, incestuous tendency—kinship libido—is a variation of the so-called primitive approach as he understands it (1946, pars. 431–49). The tendencies that abolish structure in incestuous union (endogamy) and create it through collective representations of order (exogamy) balance one another. Jung found that inner structure must be created and then led back toward kinship and relationship with others. Jung says that the kinship libido, "being and instinct, wants the *human* connection. That is the core of the whole transference phenomenon, and it is impossible to argue it away, because relationship to the self is at once relationship to our fellow man, and no one can be related to the latter until he is related to himself" (1946, par. 445). The emphasis in "The Psychology of the Transference" is upon first creating an inner Self structure through taking back projections and then entering into relationships. I am exaggerating this, because Jung certainly also represents it as a mutual process. But my intention is to emphasize what I regard as crucial to our understanding of the transference/countertransference process. Kinship libido is neither released nor satisfied in the manner Jung suggests. The imaginally experienced *coniunctio* that arises from the unconscious and is discovered (often later) in dreams, pales considerably when compared to its experience as a here and now reality. Its occurrence is synchronistic, an act of grace. Only by understanding its potential to dissolve and create structure simultaneously in a space outside of time that leads back into time can we grasp the allure of sexual acting-out in analysis. With this, we can also better grasp the archetypal underpinnings of this behavior.

Jung's approach, which strongly favors the priority of creating inner structure along the model of taking back projections and only then returning to kinship needs, is perhaps an ostensibly safe approach to the archetypal energies of the *coniunctio*. But it has drawbacks. On the one hand, it undermines the nature of liminality and its mystery. On the other, it casts its precious product, *communitas,* into the dangerous realm of being only a tantalizing object. In a sense, Jung opens the door to the archetypal mystery of the transference/countertransference process and then slams it shut. To see this, consider his treatment of "The King and Queen" in the *Rosarium* (see fig. 5).

There is a left-hand "sinister contact," but the secret, Jung tells us, "lies in the union of the *right* hands, for, as the figure shows, this is mediated by the *donum Spiritus Sancti*" (1946, par. 411). This indicates the need for a spiritual, transcendent link to avoid sexual acting-out, to which the "sinister" contact could lead. And here Jung makes a remarkable statement. The tantric, left-hand path, he tells us, is the path of the "'lower' spirit [of] the Primordial Man, hermaphroditic by nature . . . who was imprisoned in Physis. . . . He is man's totality, which is beyond the division of the sexes. . . . The revelation of this higher meaning solves the problems created by the 'sinister contact'" (1946, par. 416). He continues: "The revelation of the Anthropos is associated with no ordinary religious emotion; it signifies much the same thing as the vision of Christ for the believing Christian. Nevertheless it does not appear *ex opere divino,* but *ex opere naturae;* not from above but from the transformation of a shade from Hades, akin to evil itself and bearing the name of the pagan god of revelation" (1946, par. 416). Thus the most holy, spiritual contact with the *numinosum,* the ascent experience of the *unio mystica,* is brought into substantial identity with the experience of the Anthropos. The path is different, but one is approaching the same energies. And it is clear that Jung recognizes that neither can substitute for the other—both are necessary. In such amplifications, he opens the door to the archetypal levels of the transference/countertransference process.

It is my experience that women especially know the Dionysian energies that appear from nature as a transformation of the darkest mysterious depths. But frequently I have discovered that whereas a woman may deeply know these energies, she may almost have given up on ever experiencing them in a good, creative way. When I felt these energies stirring with a woman recently, and we spoke of them, I used the term sexuality to describe them. She recoiled, saying, "That isn't sexuality, it's me!" Women have often split off from this level out of extreme fear that nothing but rejection will follow. Mixed in is a great fear of verbal and physical attack. It is also very common to find that a woman fears these energies are psychotic, for that is how she experienced herself treated whenever they stirred. And, to note one more common situation, a woman will often hide these energies, even from herself, with splitting defenses because she fears they will be reduced to infantile, incestuous components by a patriarchal psychology. I think the mishandling of the energies of Hades or Pluto by men contributes more to a woman's distrust of male psychological systems than any other single factor. For a woman deeply knows, generally far more deeply than a man, the transforming, life-giving, and mystery-sustaining nature of the underworld Gods and Goddesses.

Having told us of the Anthropos and described the numinous depths that can be revealed, and how they are similar to spiritual revelations from above, as in Christianity, Jung quickly leaves this potential heresy for a structural analysis. He turns away from the left- and right-hand contacts, especially from the left-hand path, and switches to the need to integrate these issues as anima and animus projections. Here we lose the Anthropos, the Gods of the underworld, Dionysos and Hades.

Jung gives us the following description of possible relationships between a man and a woman:

(a) An uncomplicated personal relationship.
(b) A relationship of the man to his anima and of the woman to her animus.
(c) A relationship of anima to animus and *vice versa.*
(d) A relationship of the woman's animus to the man (which happens when the woman is identical with her animus), and of the man's anima to the woman (which happens when the man is identical with his anima). (1946, par. 423)

We only recover the Anthropos and the hermaphroditic being when we add a fifth relationship. This relationship is based on the woman's awareness of an inner animus, through which she is a channel for Dionysian-like energies that she extends toward the man; he meanwhile is aware of his inner anima, is a receiver of "her" energies, and extends these, now linked with her own spirit, back toward the woman. In a sense the woman's state is Yang, within which resides a Yin element, and the man is more Yin, with the Yang aspect within. Each is released back toward the other. This configuration is, then, the reverse of the physical state of affairs.

This fifth type of relationship occurs in the imaginally experienced *coniunctio* between two people, and it describes the nature of their sexuality. One item needs special mention. Since the woman's sexuality is generally more active, or at least initiating, she can be experienced by the man as a phallic mother. In turn, he can be experienced as her father was prior to the oedipal transit, at a stage where she allowed these energies to extend to him and where they were often denied or psychically abused. As a phallic mother, a woman can constellate a man's past experiences of instrusion and psychic rape. Thus the energies of the *coniunctio* stir up pre-oedipal issues. The quest for the *coniunctio* experience, however, is strongly motivated by the healing that can come to these layers of psyche just through the *coniunctio* experience. Not a few instances of sexual acting-out are the result of male analysts sensing a woman's Dionysian energies and unconsciously desiring redemption through them. A particularly offensive variant of the trickster shadow here occurs when the man casts himself as the woman's initiator, whereas in fact she is initiating him.

In the fifth type of relationship, which I have outlined, projections gain a new, outer reality. In a sense, this is a return to animism on a psychological level. It is a relationship envisioned by Ferenzci and championed by Norman Brown in *Life Against Death* (1959, p. 315). Here "matter" again gains its own life. This is actually close to Jung's attitudes, as known from his writings and from numerous anecdotal stories about him. Yet it is a possibility he kept at arm's length in "The Psychology of the Transference."

It should be noted that throughout his analysis of the alchemical imagery of the *Rosarium* and other alchemical texts pertinent to his study of the transference, Jung (1946) always sees the body as a symbol for something else. The body may symbolize the old personality (par. 478), the Great Mother (par. 480), a stage in which contents of the psyche are to be made "real" and brought to bear upon behavior (par. 486), a stage in which the consolidated Self must join with feeling in relationships (pars. 489–91), or the ego (par. 501). While in other works Jung is open to the idea of a subtle body and its partly physical, partly psychic nature, and even shows a mastery of this idea in his Nietzsche seminars (1934–39, Pt. 3, Lecture 8), in "The Psychology of the Transference" it is taken as an example of the alchemist's immature mind (1946, pars. 498–499). This loss of body and of subtle body is the price paid for the security of the path of projection analysis. It is a way that tends to split mind and body, and it runs counter to the very nature of liminality. I believe it also tends to frustrate *communitas*.

Often we do not have to impose structure any more than we have to work from a projection model of creating psychic structure. Wisdom can emerge from the *coniunctio*, and in that wisdom and its sacred space much becomes integrated (Turner 1974, pp. 266–67). This occurs not by means of transference and resistance interpretations, which are an important part of the preliminal state, but by means of simple reflection within the larger context of the archetypal transference and its central image, the *coniunctio*.

Further Reflections and Some Conclusions

During the past few years there have been a number of important statements regarding the danger to therapy and the abuse to the soul caused by sexual acting-out in the transference/countertransference. There have also been a flurry of books on Jung's life that pertain to this theme, especially the publication of the Spielrein diaries. These works have further placed this issue into central focus. In this essay, I have attempted to understand the archetypal underpinnings of sexual acting-out because I sense there is much more in it than issues of the analyst's lack of impulse control, his untamed aggression, his narcissistic invulnerability fantasies, or his energy-laden schizoid sectors thirsting for integration and being seduced by the mystery of sexuality and by dark fascinations stemming from the hermaphroditic Self. More too is involved than the awesome residual power of wounds stemming from personal and archetypal attacks upon incest desires in childhood, wounds that the analyst may attempt to heal in his patient's womb. Beyond these factors there is envy of the primal scene, which, as Melanie Klein has told us, can stem from a child's fantasy of being ripped out of a blissful union that is then transferred to the parental union and believed to stay there, forever unavailable. The excitement that often derives from and precedes sexual acting-out, the compulsion and emptiness that often follow, the despair and sadism it unleashes by the analyst's often cool, narcissistic withdrawal, are all workings of primal scene envy. We also should not fail to note that the *coniunctio* can be assimilated and used by a negative mother complex. A deficit in the mother-child union, especially the lack of a positive symbiosis, can lead to the kind of autistic behavior that is often a part of sexual acting-out, where symbolic awareness vanishes.

The very act of psychotherapy, which is a strange endeavor of two people mutually constellating the unconscious, has magnificent potential for healing as well as inherent danger. Concern with the danger involved has ruled much of our approach to the transference. I have explained how Jung regarded the hermaphroditic Self image as extremely negative in his work on the transference. I have also noted how his attitude toward the body is more anti-body in "The Psychology of the Transference" than in his other writings. Fear of the shadow potential easily leads to a loss of body, of sexuality, and of the beauty of a conjoined, hermaphroditic Self image.

It is reasonable to assume that as part of our archaic heritage we are all primed for liminal acts. We are both privy and prey to archetypal experiences in which liminal acts, such as sexual acting-out, have a positive context in rite and ritual. We need to keep in mind, therefore, the potency of the release mechanisms for liminal experience. It is highly questionable, moreover, if human beings can reach their full potential without liminal experience. We must reflect on the act of sexual acting-out against this archetypal background from which, at least in part—and I believe in strong measure—it stems.

Sexual acting-out in psychotherapy is an offense to the soul. But to avoid the liminality to which the transference/countertransference *coniunctio* can lead is also a betrayal. We need to educate ourselves to the imaginal nature of the *coniunctio* so that we will be in a position to integrate this shadow of our profession. Only then will we have a chance for transformation rather than repression, and only then will we respect the mystery of both sexuality and spirit, body and soul.

To meet the challenge of the *coniunctio* and of liminality, we need to develop the imagination, which is the capacity, as Blake said, to "see through our eyes, not with them" (Domrosch 1980, p. 15). In analysis we are called upon to develop this faculty in an embodied manner with another person.

If we can achieve integration of the dark side of the *coniunctio*—that is, if we can experience a tendency toward sexual acting-out and recognize its value as a signal that the energies necessary for the *coniunctio* have not yet been sufficiently constellated and certainly not integrated—we will not require moralistic injunctions for our guidelines. If we develop our imagination in an embodied manner, in the here and now with another person, we will gain the capacity to see imaginally the imagery of the *coniunctio* in a space between ourselves and the other, and also to know when it is *not* present, at least not for us to see. In this way, the shadow can become an ally.

One last point. The kinship libido Jung regards as an instinct reaches beyond the individual psyche. It requires more than relationship among individuals: It requires community. It is probable that the energies of *communitas* will be safely and sanely approached only where a sense of community exists. Perhaps our imaginal encounters in therapy will release the *communitas* that will engender the community we need, which perhaps alone can level us all into brethren and stem the ugly tide of narcissistic power seeking. Perhaps this community will be able to nurture the soul in such a way that sexual acting-out can be seen, against the background of the need for *communitas,* as simply a foolish act.

References

Brown, N. 1959. *Life against death.* Middletown, Conn.: Wesleyan University Press.

Domrosch, L. 1980. *Symbol and truth in Blake's myth.* Princeton: Princeton University Press.

Fordham, M. 1957. *New developments in analytical psychology.* London: Routledge and Kegan Paul.

_____. 1974. Jung's conception of transference. *The Journal of Analytical Psychology* 19/1:1–21.

Hannah, B. 1976. *Jung: His life and work.* New York: G. P. Putnam's Sons.

Henderson, J. 1982. Countertransference. *The San Francisco Library Journal* 3:48–51.

Jung, C. G. 1934–39. Psychological analysis of Nietzsche's Zarathustra. Unpublished seminar notes. Recorded and mimeographed by Mary Foote.

_____. 1946. The psychology of the transference. In *Collected works,* 16:163–323. Princeton: Princeton University Press, 1966.

_____. 1949. The psychology of the child archetype. In *Collected works,* 9/1:149–81. Princeton: Princeton University Press, 1971.

_____. 1953. *Psychology and alchemy.* In *Collected works,* vol. 12. Princeton: Princeton University Press, 1968.

_____. 1955. *Mysterium coniunctionis.* In *Collected works,* vol. 14. Princeton: Princeton University Press, 1970.

_____. 1961. Seven sermons to the dead. In *Memories, dreams, reflections,* pp. 378–90. New York: Random House.

_____. 1973. *Letters: 1906–1950,* vol. 1, G. Adler, ed. Princeton: Princeton University Press.

Schwartz-Salant, N. 1982. *Narcissism and character transformation: The psychology of narcissistic character disorders.* Toronto: Inner City Books.

Stein, R. 1974. *Incest and human love.* Baltimore: Penguin Books.

Taylor, C. 1982. Sexual intimacy between patient and analyst. *Quadrant* 15:47–54.

Turner, V. 1974. *Dramas, fields, and metaphors.* Ithaca, N.Y.: Cornell University Press.

Ulanov, A. 1979. Follow-up treatment in cases of patient/therapist sex. *Journal of the American Academy of Psychoanalysis* 7:101–10.

Zabriskie, B. 1982. Incest and myrrh: Father-daughter sex in therapy. *Quadrant* 15/2:5-24.

Dreams and Transference/ Countertransference: The Transformative Field

James A. Hall

> . . . the true physician does not stand out-
> side his work but is always in the thick of it.
>
> Jung

There should be no difficulty, theoretically, in discussing transference and countertransference in relation to the Jungian theory of
dreams. Transference is one of the oldest terms in psychoanalytic
discourse, clearly discernible in Freud's work in 1912 (pp. 97–108)
and having antecedents earlier. Jungian dream theory has many
ramifications, but they can be easily related to other schools of
depth psychology and, to some degree, to the laboratory study of
sleep and dreams (Hall 1977, pp. 3–110). What then *is* the difficulty?

The difficulty in relating these areas reaches to the very foundations of depth psychology, both Jungian and otherwise, for at the

James A. Hall, M.D., is clinical associate professor of psychiatry, University of
Texas Health Science Center, Dallas. He is a founding member and former president
of the Inter-Regional Society of Jungian Analysts and is president of the Isthmus
Institute, a non-profit foundation that sponsors annual dialogues on convergences of
science and religion. A graduate of the C. G. Jung Institute of Zurich, he is the author
of *Clinical Uses of Dreams: Jungian Interpretations and Enactments* (1977) and
Jungian Dream Interpretation: A Handbook of Theory and Practice (1983).

unconscious depths of transference/countertransference[1] (which I will often abbreviate T/CT) we face the same enigma as in considering some of the (by no means rare) phenomenology of dreams, as, for example, telepathic or parapsychological dreams (Hall 1977, p. 322) or dreams that compensate some content *other than* the dominant ego-image, as dreams of children that may compensate stresses in the family or dreams that reveal the nature of objective reality, as the famous ouroboric-snake vision of Kekule suggesting to him the chemical structure of the benzene ring.

The dilemma is this: There is no privileged position from which one can observe (without interaction effects) the psyche of another individual. All observation of the psyche (of oneself or of another) is participant observation, whether the observation is of the clinical interaction of T/CT or of the dreams of the analysand or the analyst.

This irreducible relativity of data causes no difficulty in ordinary clinical practice where transference distortions are usually so gross that the interpretation of dreams or of T/CT is essentially unambiguous (see, e.g., Hall 1977, pp. 224–30). But in crucial situations it may be extremely difficult to make a clear determination. If T/CT is considered a ratio of the relative pressures of distortions arising from transference (T) and countertransference (CT) in the transformative field of the analytic interaction, the difficulty of discrimination increases as the T/CT ratio approaches one, for then the distortions of the analyst are such that they may not be discriminated from those of the analysand, making interpretation of the analysand's material difficult. If the ratio T/CT becomes notably less than one, the analytic temenos is lost through excessive countertransference distortions. When the ratio of T/CT is significantly greater than one (the usual situation), ordinary analytical work, which is facilitative of the transformative individuation of the analysand, is possible, even though some countertransference distortions may be present.

For useful analytical work to progress, therefore, the countertransference distortions that are always present must be relatively insignificant compared with any transference distortions of the analyst in the mind of the analysand. We no longer have the luxury of Freud's early view that analysands distort their perceptions of the

---

1. I prefer in most instances to write of transference/countertransference to indicate the field quality of the unconscious interaction between analysand and analyst. The unsatisfactory nature of the terms transference and countertransference is one theme of the present discussion.

analyst, while the analyst is able to maintain a reality stance in relation to the patient.

The Transformative Field of the Analytic Relationship

Both transference and countertransference are inevitable parts of the analytic process, as is clear in Jung's major statement on this question, "The Psychology of Transference" (1946, pars. 353–539). In this essay, particularly as evidenced in the alchemical illustrations, Jung clearly shows that in any significant analytical interaction, both the analyst and the analysand are deeply involved. Therefore, either or both may be transformed by the interactions. It seems appropriate to refer to this as a *transformative field* without specification as to whether it is the analysand or the analyst who is most likely to transform. Indeed, both are likely to do so.

The major vectors of possible change in the analytical situation follow the various permutations of relationship between the analyst and analysand. Briefly stated, these are:

1. The conscious relationship of the analyst and the analysand, their therapeutic "contract" which is largely at the level of conscious ego involvement and is the basic container (temenos, vas) of the situation. This relationship contains, but is not limited to, time and place of meeting, fee structure, stated goals of analysis, etc.

2. The relationship between the conscious mind of each participant and the unconscious mind of the other. This is most easily stated in classical Jungian analytic usage as the relation of the ego of the patient to the anima of the male analyst (or the animus of the female analyst), together with the relation of the ego of the analyst to the unconscious (anima/animus) of the patient.

3. The relationship between the unconscious aspects of both the analyst and the analysand. In classical language this is often equivalent to anima-animus forms of interaction, characterized by their predominance of abstract and non-personal elements, although such interaction may *feel* personal and emotionally related.

4. The inner relationship between the conscious and unconscious mind of the patient; the similar relationship between the conscious and unconscious mind of the analyst. This is *the* vital interaction within each person of the dyad, for it is the movement toward integration of the conscious and unconscious parts of the *person* that is the essence of the individuation process. The other

interactions may be considered ancillary to safe and effective facilitation of this integration.

A great deal of the work of the analyst is to maintain the analytical situation as a transformative field in which the individuative transformation of the analysand is more likely to take place. This is very similar to the containing quality of the analytic relationship that Winnicott (1951) has emphasized. When the structure of the transformative field is threatened with dissolution or imbalance, its repair must take precedence over the usual activity of analysis, such as dream interpretation.

A modification of Jung's diagram (1946, par. 422) may make these statements even clearer (see fig. 1). I have altered the diagram slightly, substituting *analyst* for *adept* and *analysand* for *soror*, the mystical "sister" and female assistant of the male alchemist (1976, par. 1703). Also, I have taken the liberty to add some subscripts to the letters used to designate the interactions; this is for ease of reference in our present discussion. Anima and animus are listed in their original position and terminology, but it should be remembered that each stands here in the role of psychopomp or guide to the unconscious, so that they are fulfilling a functional role that might at times be performed by another structural component of the

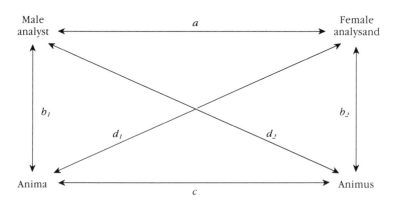

Figure 1. a = the conscious relationship; b_1 = the analyst's relationship with his unconscious; b_2 = the analysand's relationship with her unconscious, a principal focus of the work of analysis; c = the unconscious relationship between the anima of the analyst and the animus of the female analysand; d_1 = the animus of the analysand in relation to the conscious ego of the analyst; d_2 = the anima of the analyst in relation to the conscious ego of the analysand. (Adapted from C. G. Jung, "The Psychology of the Transference." In *Collected Works*, 16:221. Princeton: Princeton University Press. © 1966 by Princeton University Press. Reprinted by permission.)

psyche, such as the Self. Anima/animus in this sense stands for the entire relationship of ego-consciousness with the unconscious.[2] The assumption of a male analyst and a female analysand is arbitrary, of course, and could be reversed, or both persons might be of the same sex.

The conscious relationship (a) is the intentional and official interaction of the analytical process, while b_1 and b_2 represent the conscious/unconscious relationship *within* the analyst and the analysand, respectively, the line along which the basic individuation of each takes place. The crossed relationships d_1 and d_2 represent the forms of interaction between the consciousness of one person of the dyad and the unconscious of the other. It is expected that d_1 is part of the ordinary transference distortion described by Freud, while d_2 should be minimal, although both of these crossed relationships must always be present to some degree in the transformative field of the analysis. The unconscious relationship c is always present, but in it neither analyst nor analysand is sufficiently conscious to offer ego support for the process, which is not necessarily undesirable or untransformative simply because it is unconscious.

The proper functioning of the analysis requires certain conditions that can be roughly represented in this diagram. The conscious containing qualities of the relationship must always be able to withstand the unconscious pressure of both the analyst and the analysand: The strength of the first grouping of ($a + b_1 + b_2$) must be greater than the pressure of the second grouping of ($d_1 + d_2 + c$). I propose to refer to the first grouping by the term temenos because it is used in Jungian literature and because it retains more of the archetypal flavor than the clinical word *container* or Winnicott's word *holding;* it refers to much the same quality and is analogous to the alchemical vas. The second grouping ($d_1 + d_2 + c$) is really the *prima materia* of transformation for *both* the analyst and the analysand, but I do not at present think that it is useful to propose a specific name for it.

Some Case Examples

Years ago in (mercifully) the early days of my career as an analyst, I saw a young, neurotic woman for a brief period of therapy

---

2. Although discussion of anima/animus is not relevant to our main concerns here, it is important to state that in my own understanding these terms refer primarily to the function of relationship designed to enlarge the sphere of the personal rather than to any assigned content such as "soul" or "spirit" (cf. Hall 1983, pp. 16-18).

that never reached the stage of analysis. After a number of visits over a few months, she said to me at the beginning of a session, "*You* know what's wrong with me and I don't. Besides, I haven't much money. Why don't you tell me what's wrong with me so that I can work faster and save what little money I have?" I responded (incorrectly) to this as if it were a communication only on level a, but it was soon apparent that the bulk of the energy was from d_1, the patient's animus talking "logic" to my ego. "All right," I said, "I'll tell you," and proceeded to list a number of (to me) obvious things that would need to be altered for her to be somewhat free of her neurotic depression. She took these in a way entirely different from what I had assumed was level a communication. I had hardly finished the short listing when she angrily slammed her purse on my desk and then stormed out of the office, saying "If *that's* the way you feel, I'm leaving!" I did not hear from her for another three months, after which she came back for a brief period and did some useful work on her neurosis.

Dreams of either the analysand or the analyst not infrequently speak to the T/CT aspects of analysis. At these times, it is most crucial to differentiate to whatever degree is possible the objective from the subjective meanings of the dreams.

I have discussed previously (Hall 1977, pp. 229–30) the dream of a young student who suffered from oedipal problems, one symptom of which was his feeling of never being able to do anything as "good as you [the analyst] do it." While in these neurotic self-deprecating feelings, he dreamed that he and I were in joint search of "the source," which proved to be an artesian fountain of light. At times in the dream he was leading me; at times I was ahead and calling back to him: a clear symbol of the analytical endeavor being a joint search in which no one had already achieved the goal. In terms of the diagram of the transformative field, his dream reminded him that a and d_1 did not predominate. In fact, all the relations of the diagram can be found in the dream.

A woman whose teenage daughter was treated for anorexia nervosa came to complain that I was not pursuing the correct treatment as outlined in a (rather good) popular book she had been reading about the problem of anorexia. She brought the book with her to further my education. It was only after we had talked through the issues and achieved some degree of consensus that she told me a dream she had recently experienced. In the dream I (the analyst) was driving a convertible car with other people in it, but I was not driving too well, bumping into walls, running over gardens, etc., which—if objective—would raise serious questions about the treatment plan I had proposed. But then she added that "the car didn't get damaged when it hit the walls" because it "seemed to bounce back" and in spite of all the erratic driving "we were getting there, we were getting to where we wanted to go."

The analyst's dreams may make him sensitive to countertransference or transference distortions. The dream of a white rhinoceros (Hall 1977, pp. 226–27) threatening both the analyst and the patient revealed to an analyst that both he and the analysand were threatened by an autonomous complex that might belong to either of them or to both, a danger discussed by Meier (1959, p. 28). In the dream, the T/CT conflict was not to be settled by a legal process (deciding whose complex it was), but it could be safely handled if both of them watched for its activity. The analyst did not discuss the dream with the patient, but it afforded the analyst a perspective from which to deal with an impasse that might otherwise have prematurely ended the psychotherapy process. This dream was pointing essentially to an activity of level c, specifically suggesting the avoidance of the crossed-relationship d_1 and d_2, and emphasizing the value of the conscious relationship a. Both partners of the analytical dyad needed to pay attention to their own unconscious processes (b_1 and b_2), which were similar.

Although I feel that it is generally best for the analyst not to discuss with the patient the dreams of the analyst that include the patient, it is important that the analyst act upon his understanding of the dream, as in the white rhinoceros dream cited above. Machtiger (1982, p. 106), however, has pointed out that there are recorded instances of Jung sharing his dreams with patients (Jung 1961b, p. 133). My own reasoning is this: The dream can be taken as "deeper" than the ego understanding (and often it is deeper), so that sharing a dream of someone with the person himself may invite him to project his own understanding (correct or incorrect) into the dream, feeling that he knows more the "true" feelings of the dreamer-analyst than the analyst says. Consider, for example, a nonanalytical example of the danger of projection in sharing a dream. A woman shared with her husband a dream in which she was riding in a car with two male members of her psychotherapy group, but the husband projected his own fears into the dream and accused her of having sexual feelings, if not relations, with the two men. He assimilated her dream to his own structure of complexes. It seems to me important to understand and responsibly to act on any dream in which a patient appears, although it is not usually best to share the dream with the patient.

The most common T/CT effect of a dream is similar to that cited by Jung above (1961b, p. 133), in which the dream compensates in a positive or negative way a distortion of the image of the other person in the waking ego. In Jung's example, his own dream of having to look *up* to his patient seemed to compensate his unnoticed tendency to look *down* on her. Such dream compensations of excessive idealization or negation of the other person tend to restore the symmetrical relationship of the transformative field where *both* analysand and analyst are involved in transformation, even though it may be at different rates of speed and in different forms. A striking example of compensation of a strong negative transference onto me by a woman with many neurotic and reality problems occurred in two short dreams of hers several nights apart:

Dreams:
> *You [the analyst] were lecturing to a group of people including me [the dream-ego]. You stopped and said you were dying of cancer and I cried.*

> *I was with you [the analyst] and was happy. I may have even kissed you lightly, but not sexually. I felt warm toward you because you were willing to let me unravel and act out without rejecting me.*

The patient who had these two positive dreams, with the slight erotic overtone in the second, had become furious at me on many occasions, had broken off therapy abruptly at least once, blaming me for her decision to do so, and had generally (it seemed) expressed to me all the hostility which she had been unable to voice to her mother, hostility that also stemmed from the death of one of her own children and the severe incapacity of another. The dreams helped to redress the imbalance of her negative transference, helping her to make more use of the psychotherapy she needed.

Dreams and T/CT: Some Guidelines

Whenever the analyst appears in the dreams of an analysand, it is even more important than usual to elicit all associations to the dream. *Is* there any hidden feeling toward the analyst, positive or negative, that the patient has known of but has not expressed, possibly because of transference fears of retaliation or rejection? Secondly, the analyst should ask himself if the patient's dream might possibly be objective, referring to the analyst directly and not to the analyst as the personification of a part of the patient's own unconscious mind (a not-infrequent meaning of the analyst-in-the-dream). As the patient begins to improve, the analyst-in-the-dream may represent the newly acquired insight derived from analysis.

When the analyst dreams of the patient, it is most important for the analyst to understand if he has made distortions of the patient, perhaps overvaluing or undervaluing the analysand. If necessary, the analyst should discuss the dream (in some instances, the entire case) with a colleague or with the analyst's own analyst. In most instances, the analyst himself will be able to understand his dream and make appropriate movements within the analysis to correct any distortions of the patient's material. Only in rare instances, and with forethought, should the analyst consider discussing directly with the patient one of his own dreams of the patient.

When there is insufficient appreciation of the archetypal levels of the T/CT, there is sometimes pressure to interpret dream images as referring to the T/CT when there is no supporting evidence in the dream itself. If we consider dreams to be self-representations of the psyche, elaborated in compensation to the view of the dominant ego-image, the dreams are perfectly capable of presenting the analyst himself in the dream when they are emphasizing an objective meaning. Figures other than the analyst in dreams should, in my opinion, only rarely be considered to refer to the analyst, since the dream from a Jungian view is not "disguised"—there is no need to substitute another figure for the analyst himself. Instead dreams are symbolic; many dream figures may refer to the same core of complexes, groups of images related by a common emotional tone, as a negative father-complex, for example. What one *does* find in dreams are recurrent patterns, those chosen by the Self to present the dream-ego with opportunities to alter the complex structure of the mind, upon which the waking-ego relies for much of its sense of identity (Hall 1977, pp. 141–79; 1982). The analyst may appear in a patient's dream as one of several images representing a particular complex structure in various of its nuances and relationships to other structural components of the patient's psyche. When the image of the analyst does appear, of course, it is important to give somewhat greater weight to the possibility of objective interpretation, although it is best if all dream images are first considered primarily as subjective.

Erotic Problems

Nothing seems to arouse as much affect in discussion of analysis as erotic feelings between analysand and analyst and the danger of their being acted upon, with the involvement of important ethical, moral, and legal considerations as well as analytical ones. It should be simply stated that sexual feelings between analyst and analysand are to be expected, just as in any other in-depth relationship. This may mean simply sexual attractiveness on the ego-level, as might occur between any two persons with or without a personal relationship. The analytical temenos contains a relationship of doctor and patient that "remains a personal one within the impersonal framework of professional treatment" (Jung 1966a, par. 163). All the feelings of personal relationship, including sexual feelings, may arise, but they are modified by the professional setting and temenos.

Sexual dreams, therefore, must be handled most carefully when the sexual object is the analyst in a patient's dream or the patient in the dream of an analyst. Self-disclosure by the analyst of sexual feelings for a patient is one of the most difficult technical areas in analysis: It can relieve transference pressures by indicating that they have some basis in reality or it may (but does not inevitably) inflame the erotic transference to a dangerous level.

In the early days of my practice, I was sure that a particularly attractive woman patient was having sexual feelings for me. She said nothing overtly, nor were there sexual dreams. She did finger the fountain pen of my desk writing set in what seemed to me an erotic way, almost as if stroking a penis. Our analytical work ended because of external circumstances, her leaving on an extended trip and my being "invited" to join the army during the Vietnam conflict. A few weeks after she departed, I received a package from her. It was an old copy of Graham Greene's novel *The End of the Affair*, mailed without comment, as if it needed one! In retrospect, I feel that it was a technical error not to introduce the question of erotic T/CT feelings for discussion. They were apparently much nearer the surface of her consciousness than I had judged.

A second very attractive woman patient had a long series of erotic dreams about me, although claiming to have no conscious sexual feelings. I was aware of my own sexual fantasies about her, but continued to interpret the dreams in a subjective manner, as if the sexual feelings referred to a *coniunctio* symbol of uniting her ego with her animus (relationship b_2). The erotic dreams continued unabated. I discussed the situation with the analyst with whom I had done the bulk of my control work and he said (wisely, I think) that her unconscious simply might be interested in knowing whether I in reality had sexual feelings toward her, since her dreams had failed to alter course with repeated subjective interpretations. With fear and anxiety, I told her of my sexual thoughts when she next brought erotic transference dreams, adding that there was a clear distinction between feeling and action, that I had no intention of acting on such feelings or being seductive, since the value of the analytical process was more important than the erotic feelings. She hardly reacted at all, simply acknowledging that she understood that I might have sexual feelings and that she, too, valued the progress she was making in analysis. As if in response to the disclosure, her dreams immediately dropped the erotic transference theme and began dealing with other more pressing areas of the analytic process. In this instance, my supervisor's advice was correct and the self-disclosure (with attendant safeguarding statements) was appropriate and effective.

Erotic transference dreams may be a symbolic attempt to establish a connection with the analyst where there is insufficient emotional involvement (Jung 1966*a*, par. 276; 1976, par. 333). Jung (1946, pars. 353–529) also recognized the more archetypal meaning of sexual transference, which would seem to be in the service of *coniunctio* (the union of opposites) and transformation and should not be simply reduced to a personalistic meaning of sexual attraction.

There is danger, of course, in concretizing a sexual transference, acting upon it, and losing the temenos of analysis. Excessive sexual interpretation of unconscious material may promote an erotic transference (Jung 1966*a*, par. 273). I know directly, however, of only four instances in which a therapist (not necessarily an analyst) was sexually involved with a patient. These instances were told to me by the therapist involved and I have no reason to doubt them. I know *of* other instances and read of them in the literature. In these four of which I have some direct understanding, the sex of the involved therapists is equally split: two male therapists involved with female patients and two female therapists involved with male patients. There was, I believe, a positive outcome of the involvement in two cases, one with a female, one with a male therapist. The instance of the other male therapist was a disaster for both patient and therapist, while the fourth outcome, so far as I know it, was indifferent. It is difficult to say that one person seduced another in these instances. If there was a clear seduction in one case, it was the seduction of a male therapist by a female analysand, but there were so many levels of that relationship that it is difficult to know if it belongs in the usual discussion of T/CT interaction. I believe that our ethical standards opposed to sexual involvements in analysis are quite correct, but I do not think that when such cases occur, we should immediately judge the analyst the guilty party, except perhaps in repetitive or characterological cases. This is such a sensitive issue, practically and theoretically, that we should use all our understanding to delve into the *meaning* of an involvement rather than immediately judge when we know of its occurrence. Much more data of an *analytical nature* is needed, and there are many obvious obstacles to its impartial collection. I do not know if the four cases of which I can speak with some analytical understanding are typical, but they are enough to suggest caution in making interpretations of such involvements. The traditional argument that one must not "act out" so that libido will activate images instead of actions is essentially a circular argument, allowing one to argue the opposite: that "acting out" might begin the flow of libido when it is insufficient. We must examine these questions with due caution and reserve.

Jungian and Other Views

The most recent overview of the Jungian approach to T/CT is available in *Jungian Analysis* (Stein, ed. 1982) in excellent papers in that volume by Ulanov, Machtiger, and McCurdy. Fordham (1979) has made a number of contributions to the understanding of T/CT, with the special emphasis of the London group on analysis of the transference and on reductive analysis. His contribution is well reviewed by Machtiger, while McCurdy calls attention to the interesting study of T/CT imagery during therapy sessions as reported by Dieckmann (1976), who was in charge of such research in the Berlin Institute. In addition, Groesbeck (1978) has emphasized the influence of personality typology in the analysis of the transference.

There remains a vast difference between the Jungian views of T/CT and those writers in other areas of depth psychology. The principle differences are (a) the Jungian understanding of the archetypal and transpersonal aspects of T/CT, and (b) what I have called the *transformative field*, the inevitable mutual participation of the analyst and analysand in a process that is greater than either of them, as in the dream of the "source" as a fountain of light.

There are attempts to approach the archetypal and transformative aspects of T/CT outside the framework of Jungian psychology. Denes (1980) speaks of a "bipolar field" instead of T/CT, a term similar to Langs's "bipersonal field." Both terms focus on the dyad of analyst/analysand and slight the archetypal foundations. Dysart (1977) appreciates how change can take place with little or no insight by the patient. The patient is also recognized as a participant observer of the process, together with the analyst (Wolstein 1977). There is a growing understanding that T/CT needs to be understood as a field phenomenon, but Jung is seldom mentioned, credit most often being given to the later concept of "parataxis" introduced by Harry Stack Sullivan (Searles 1977). There is understanding of the stress on the analyst of maintaining the transformative field in spite of transference attacks by the analysand (Schaefer 1977, 1982). Hunt (1978) suggests seeing T/CT as an open system composed of interacting subsystems. Many agree with Chrzanowski (1979) that T/CT transcends the traditional concept of transference and its interpretation. It is clear that there is a groping for a reformulation of T/CT, but a groping generally uninformed by the Jungian vision.

One of the most compatible statements with Jungian thought is the paper by Wachtel(1980) relating T/CT to the Piagetian concepts of *schema, assimilation,* and *accommodation.* Schemata are constructed through the child's interaction with the environment, although there are tendencies to form certain types of patterns, particularly where perception is concerned. This parallels the Jungian *complex,* which is formed from personal interaction with the world, but based upon archetypal forms; the complex may include archetypal images and personal images, but the core of the complex is the archetype itself—the pure tendency to structure experience in certain ways. There may be patterns or groupings of complexes, and one complex may predominate over another. These movements of complexes, reflected in images of them, can at times be seen in dreams and related to clinical changes in the waking state (Hall 1977, pp. 141–62). When new experiences occur, they can be *assimilated* (Piaget) to an existing *schema* (pattern of complexes, object-relations pattern) or the *schema* can be *accommodated* (modified) in response to the new experience. It is quite easy to see the parallels to the Jungian view, but Wachtel does not mention Jung in his excellent paper![3]

Jung's Own Views

Jung speaks of transference and countertransference throughout his *Collected Works*, but his views are concentrated in two major sources. The clinical aspects are discussed in the fifth of the Tavistock Lectures (1976, pars. 304–80), while the archetypal elements of T/CT are discussed most fully in his 1946 publication "Psychology of the Transference" (1946, pars. 353–539).

Jung (1966*a*, par. 284) defined the transference as a "number of projections which act as a substitute for a real psychological relationship," the sudden severance of which could be "unpleasant and even dangerous." Even when the resolution of the transference seems impossible, it may be brought about through the activity of the unconscious mind (1966*b*, par. 251). Jung realized (1954, par. 260) that transference was used in a larger sense than the technical sense of projection of unconscious contents from the patient's mind onto the analyst, being expanded to cover all the "exceedingly complex processes which bind the patient to the analyst." He did not find the transference *necessary* but something that must be dealt with when present (1966*b*, par. 94 n. 13), although he acknowledged that he had originally agreed with Freud that the importance of the transference could not be overestimated (1946, par. 370). The transference is produced partially through the patient's sharing his secret thoughts with the analyst (1961*a*, par. 433). Apparent cures can occur on the strength of the transference of a father imago onto the analyst (1966*b*, par. 206), but "a real settlement with the unconscious demands a firmly opposed conscious standpoint" (1966*b*, par. 342). As in other instances, it is important to distinguish between the imago of a person (the subjective relation to the object) and the object (person) as an independent reality (1971, par. 812).

The patient may have several reasons for maintaining the transference (1961*a*, par. 439), including (a) the loving attention of a father-like person, who (b) is outside the family and its constraints, and who (c) is often in reality of demonstrable therapeutic help to the analysand. This is an infantile attitude, of course, and resistance to interpretation of the transference occurs as soon as the question

---

3. I am indebted to Sally Parks for calling these parallels to my attention.

of resolving this infantile attitude arises (1961*a,* par. 657). The use of a negative transference to block insight about the infantile attitude prevents the occurrence of sufficient positive transference and its attendant symbolism, the synthesis of opposites (1946, par. 371 n. 2). The Freudian view is too personalistic and overlooks "the essence of the transference—the collective contents of an archetypal nature" (1946, par. 381, n. 34).

In a broader sense, transference is not simply to persons, but, since it is a specific form of the more general process of projection (1976, par. 312), it can also fall on physical objects (1976, par. 313; pars. 325–26) or animals (1976, par. 324). The actual therapeutic effect may derive from the analyst's efforts to enter a psychological relationship, the thing the patient is lacking (1966*a,* par. 276).

Transference can be present even before the analysis begins, based on prior acquaintance with the analyst or upon pure projection from the analysand (1976, pars. 328–29). When the projected contents fall upon a similar unconscious content in the analyst, there may be a condition of participation, which Freud described as countertransference (1976, par. 322). This is a condition of personal contamination through mutual unconsciousness (1976, pars. 323, 519).

Jung calls the transference and countertransference together *subjectivation* (1976, par. 532), a word that he does not subsequently adopt as a technical term. In this state of subjectivation, or participation, there is a danger of understanding (subjective) overbalancing knowledge (objective) to a degree that "is injurious to both partners."

The intensity of the transference is a measure of the importance to the subject of the unconscious content being transferred (1976, pars. 327, 352, 1094), which may indicate a demand for individuation (1976, par. 1097). The transference may loose unexpected archetypal figures, who are surprising because perhaps we " 'forgot the gods' " (1966*b,* par. 163). The archetypal nature of the transference is quite different from "Freudian and Adlerian reductions" because it is not a matter of simply removing impediments to more normal functioning in life, but it is a process wherein the analysand is confronted "with the task of finding a meaning that will enable him to continue living at all—a meaning more than blank resignation and mournful retrospect" (1966*b,* par. 113). The transpersonal, archetypal form of the transference may be seeking "all those potent and mighty thoughts without which man ceases to be man" (1966*b,* par. 105). The analysand may interpret archetypal images "rational-istically, in the spirit of the age" and deny what is happening (1946, par. 466).

Jung (1976, pars. 357–77) cites four stages of therapy of the transference, linking them to movement toward understanding of the archetypal elements:

1. Working through the projection of personal images.

2. Discrimination between personal and impersonal contents.

3. Differentiation of the personal relationship to the analyst from impersonal factors.

4. The objectivation of impersonal images.

The working through of these stages of personal and archetypal transference are for the purpose of detaching consciousness from the object "so that the individual no longer places the guarantee of his happiness, or of his life even, in factors outside himself, whether they be persons, ideas, or circumstances, but comes to realize that everything depends on whether he holds the treasure or not" (1976, par. 377).

Asking the patient to break the transference relationship is a significant request, since he is asked to do something that is seldom demanded of the average person, but usually only in certain reli-gious practices (1961a, par. 443). The treatment of the transference reveals "in a pitiless light what the healing agent really is: it is the degree to which the analyst himself can cope with his own psychic problems" (1976, par. 1172). The real meaning of the transference is not to be sought in its historical antecedents (by reductive analysis) but in its purpose (1969a, par. 146). The archetypal aspects of the imagery may be the attempt of the unconscious to "free a vision of God from the veils of the personal" (1966b, par. 214).

The most important outcome of the analysis of T/CT is to make the patient realize "the *subjective value* of the personal and imper-sonal contents of his transference" (1976, par. 358). Even if it were possible, it would not be right to destroy the transpersonal archety-pal images (1976, par. 360) because they are an integral part of the psyche and may have to appear in projected form to avoid inunda-tion of consciousness (1976, par. 361). What actually lies behind the transference is the patient's own potential wholeness, the Self (1969b, par. 230). When freed from the personal aspects of the transference, this may serve a religious function, leading the analy-sand to a church or religious creed (1976, par. 374) or to a personal sense of an "I-Thou" relationship if there is no acceptable transpersonal container in the outer collective world (1969*b*, par. 549).

Dreams and T/CT: Similarity of Structures

It is now possible to consider a few exploratory similarities between the structure of dreams and the structure of T/CT. Both may be important avenues toward individuation, even if experienced outside formal analysis. The dream relates the waking-ego to its own inner foundations, which can be seen as the same type of endogamous movement as T/CT, an outlet for kinship libido that has been overshadowed by the massive development of exogamous structures, which leave everyone "a stranger among strangers" (Jung 1946, par. 445; see also 1976, par. 1162). The tensions raised by the dream or by T/CT face the waking-ego with the task of relating to the unconscious, which "should be given the chance of having its way too—as much of it as we can stand"—a position that means "open conflict and open collaboration at once" (1969*a*, par. 522).

Both the dream-ego and the waking-ego under the influence of T/CT move toward what Jung (1960, par. 86 and n. 9) called an *affect-ego,* a modification of the ego-complex resulting from the emergence of a strongly toned complex. The affect-ego is in touch with and may be in danger of being overwhelmed by the activated complex. It must work to integrate the unconscious content, restore ego-stability, and maintain a sense of enduring reality. In the terms of our diagram, if the pressure is from T/CT the ego must resist an over-activity of b_2, d_1, or c, while maintaining the stabilizing quality of the interaction. If the pressure is from the unconscious itself, not involved in a T/CT situation, it must maintain a sense of ordinary ego-stability, which may at times be a heroic task, as Jung (1961*b*, p. 189) described.

In both the dream and in the situation of T/CT there is a container, a temenos or vas, in which the ordinary waking-ego is permitted to deintegrate into components and perhaps experience aspects of its own deeper nature that are not accessible in the ordinary state of ego-stability. In the dream, the temenos is the Self, as dream maker, and the ability to awaken from the affect-ego states of the dream into the relative stability of the ordinary waking-ego. In the situation of T/CT the stability is offered by the conscious relationship with the analyst (relationship *a* in the diagram). Both analysand and analyst, however, are open to the deintegration allowed in the temenos of analysis, but the analyst is more aware of the process, having experienced it in his own personal analysis, and can act as a guide to the analysand if the analyst's own unconscious processes are not overly active (relationships b_1, d_2, and c). The repeated experience of leaving the analytical situation of T/CT and returning to the "ordinary" world is analogous to repeated awakenings from the affect-ego states of the dream-ego into the stability of the characterologically stabilized waking-ego. In both instances, however, it is ultimately the Self that guarantees the stability of the ego.

The concept of affect-ego is useful to describe a stage in the transformative field that is essential to transformation of the dominant ego-image of the analysand. The affect-ego state associated with the represssed neurotic identity structure can be evoked in many ways, including group psychotherapy, which is becoming more widely appreciated by Jungians. The Inter-Regional Society, in fact, permits training candidates to list group therapy experience with an Inter-Regional analyst for up to 50 hours of the required analytic experience at a ratio of two group hours counting for one individual analytical hour. In traditional analysis, the affect-ego state is most often generated by dreams and their relation to similar structures in waking life (see Hall 1977, pp. 141–62). The T/CT interaction is another powerful generator of affect-ego states. Many other techniques may be useful at the stage of affectively experiencing different poles of the neurotic object-relations (identity-structure) pattern. These techniques can be generically described as *enactments* (Hall 1977, pp. 331–48).

The Personal Sphere and T/CT

The alchemical model of T/CT may obscure one major clinical emphasis: that the responsibility for maintaining an analytical temenos falls to a greater degree upon the analyst than upon the analysand, who need simply continue the analysis and, within that protective boundary, permit the emergence of affect-ego states that become the *prima materia* of the analysis. This asymmetry of responsibility in maintaining the temenos of analysis is not evident in the alchemical illustrations that Jung chose for his essay, "The Psychology of the Transference," illustrations that show an absolute equality of interaction between alchemist (analogous to analyst) and *soror* (analogous to analysand). [For another treatment of these alchemical illustrations, see Schwartz-Salant, pp. 1–30, in this issue. *Ed.*] These alchemical illustrations are actually a model for mutual transformation in what I would call *the personal sphere,* that range of close mutual interaction that is both the repository of unresolved problems of individuation and the psychic space in which such problems finally may be resolved. Jung's definition of the analytic relationship as being personal within the impersonal framework of professional treatment relates the concept of personal sphere (which has many applications outside of analysis) to the particular structure of analysis. The analytic relationship, to paraphrase Jung, is a personal relationship focused on the transformation of one of the parties (the analysand) within the temenos of a professional relationship in which the other party (the analyst) holds responsibilities different from those in an unframed relationship, although both formal analytic relationships and informal personal relationships may constellate part or all of a transformative field. The pressure in the analyst for the creation of a mutually personal sphere is a source of potentially disruptive countertransference reactions that can disturb the transformative field. Erotic countertransference may arise from this source, but there are clearly other forms that may be equally strong, for instance, loneliness or perhaps a sense of intellectual isolation.

Summary

An examination of T/CT leads to unexpected problems of maintaining ego-identity in transpersonal and archetypal constellations. This is analogous to some problems of dream interpretation in which it is difficult to decide between an objective and a subjective interpretation. In ordinary ranges of T/CT there is no difficulty, but analysand and analyst are always to some degree both involved in T/CT, so that there is no privileged point of view from which the psyche can be viewed without interaction distortions. Dreams of both the analyst and the analysand can be helpful in stabilizing the T/CT situation so that the conscious relationship between them, and the individuation processes in both of them, can act as a suitable temenos to contain a *transformative field* in which both analysand and analyst may be affected.

References

Chrzanowski, G. 1979. The transference-countertransference transaction. *Contemporary Psychoanalysis* 15/3:458–71.

Denes, M. 1980. Paradoxes in the therapeutic relationship. *Gestalt Journal* 3/1:41–51.

Dieckmann, H. 1976. Transference and countertransference: Results of a Berlin research group. *Journal of Analytical Psychology* 21/1:25–36.

Dysart, D. 1977. Transference cure and narcissism. *Journal of the American Academy of Psychoanalysis* 5/1:17–29.

Fordham, M. 1979. Analytical psychology and countertransference. *Contemporary Psychoanalysis* 15/4:630–46.

Freud, S. 1912. The dynamics of transference. In *Standard edition* 12:97–108. London: Hogarth Press and The Institute for Psycho-analysis.

Groesbeck, C. J. 1978. Psychological types in the analysis of the transference. *Journal of Analytical Psychology* 23/1:23–53.

Hall, J. A. 1977. *Clinical uses of dreams: Jungian interpretations and enactments.* New York and London: Grune & Stratton.

_____. 1982. Polanyi and Jungian psychology: Dream-ego and waking-ego. *Journal of Analytical Psychology* 27:239–54.

_____. 1983. *Jungian dream interpretation: A handbook of theory and practice.* Toronto: Inner City.

Hunt, W. R. 1978. The transference-countertransference system. *Journal of the American Academy of Psychoanalysis* 6/4:433–61.

Jung, C. G. 1946. The psychology of the transference. In *Collected works,* 16:163–323. Princeton: Princeton University Press, 1966.

_____. 1954. *The development of personality.* In *Collected works,* vol. 17. Princeton: Princeton University Press.

_____. 1960. *The psychogenesis of mental disease.* In *Collected works,* vol. 3. Princeton: Princeton University Press.

_____. 1961a. *Freud and psychoanalysis.* In *Collected works,* vol. 4. Princeton: Princeton University Press.

_____. 1961b. *Memories, dreams, reflections.* New York: Random House.

_____. 1966a. *The practice of psychotherapy.* In *Collected works,* vol. 16. Princeton: Princeton University Press.

_____. 1966b. *Two essays on analytical psychology.* In *Collected works,* vol. 7. Princeton: Princeton University Press.

_____. 1968. *Psychology and alchemy.* In *Collected works,* vol. 12. Princeton: Princeton University Press.

_____. 1969a. *The archetypes and the collective unconscious.* In *Collected works,* vol. 9, part 1. Princeton: Princeton University Press.

_____. 1969b. *Psychology and religion: West and east.* In *Collected works,* vol. 11. Princeton: Princeton University Press.

_____. 1969c. *The structure and dynamics of the psyche.* In *Collected works,* vol. 8. Princeton: Princeton University Press.

_____. 1970. *Civilization in transition.* In *Collected works,* vol. 10. Princeton: Princeton University Press.

_____. 1971. *Psychological types.* In *Collected works,* vol. 6. Princeton: Princeton University Press.

_____. 1976. *The symbolic life.* In *Collected works,* vol. 18. Princeton: Princeton University Press.

Machtiger, H. G. 1982. *Countertransference/transference.* In *Jungian analysis,* M. Stein, ed., pp. 86–110. La Salle, Ill., and London: Open Court.

McCurdy, A. 1981. Establishing and maintaining the analytical structure. In *Jungian analysis,* M. Stein, ed., pp. 47–67. La Salle, Ill., and London: Open Court.

Meier, C. 1959. Projection, transference and the subject-object relation in psychology. *Journal of Analytical Psychology* 4/1:21–34.

Schaefer, R. 1977. The interpretation of transference and the conditions for loving. *Journal of the American Psychoanalytical Association* 25/2:335–62.

————. 1982. The relevance of the "here and now" transference interpretation to the reconstruction of early development. *International Journal of Psycho-Analysis* 63/1:77–82.

Searles, H. F. 1977. The analyst's participation observation as influenced by the patient's transference. *Contemporary Psychoanalysis* 13/3:367–71.

————. 1979. The self in the countertransference. *Issues in Ego Psychology* 2/2:49–56.

Stein, M., ed. 1982. *Jungian analysis.* La Salle, Ill., and London: Open Court.

Ulanov, A. 1982. Transference/countertransference: A Jungian perspective. In *Jungian analysis,* M. Stein, ed., pp. 68–85. La Salle, Ill., and London: Open Court.

Wachtel, P. 1980. Transference, schema, and assimilation: The relevance of Piaget to the psychoanalytic theory of transference. In *Annual of Psychoanalysis VII,* Chicago Institute for Psychoanalysis, ed., pp. 59–76. New York: International Universities Press.

Winnicott, D. W. 1951. Transitional objects and transitional phenomena. In *Through paediatrics to psycho-analysis,* pp. 52–69. London: Hogarth.

Wolstein, B. 1977. Countertransference, counterresistance, counteranxiety: The anxiety of influence and the uniqueness of curiosity. *Contemporary Psychoanalysis* 13/1:16–29.

Transference and Countertransference in Analysis Dealing with Eating Disorders

Marion Woodman

In the Zen art of archery the arrow, if released at its highest point of tension, a tension constellated between the arrow and the bow, flies directly to its target. In analysis, the highest point of tension between analyst and analysand, depending upon the rapport between them, may constellate itself at any time. A powerful transference onto the analyst may be compared to the release of the arrow. If the transference flies wide of the mark, as it often does, the arrow is not flying on the full energy or strength of the bent bow. Then the analyst has no difficulty recognizing the transference and where psychically it is coming from. When, however, the communion of arrow and bow is such that they fuse into one (the point of highest tension), then the transference in striking home, flying to the dead center of the bull's-eye, produces a very different situation, one that is much more difficult to deal with directly because the arrow may have struck the analyst's most painful complex.

Transference in analysis often has for its true object the analyst's own point of wounding, and when it strikes home, the result inevit-

Marion Woodman is a Jungian analyst in private practice in Toronto, having received her training at the C. G. Jung Institute in Zurich. She is the author of *The Owl Was a Baker's Daughter: Obesity, Anorexia Nervosa, and the Repressed Feminine* (1980) and *Addiction to Perfection: The Still Unravished Bride* (1982).

ably is a countertransference. If the analyst is not fully aware of his or her own shadow response, real damage can be done. If, however, the analyst knows his own autonomous complex and how to deal with it (how far and no further), then the striking of it by the transference can become one of the most creative stages of the analysis, a stage in which the real work can be done. The analysand penetrates the analyst's wound (as the God enters through the wound) and what can flow from it is a healing if—and only if—the analyst has been there and dealt with it, and the analysand in the process is able to recognize that what is going on is, to use one mythical representation, fighting the Medusa by means of the mirroring shield. My image of the analyst at the end of the day is St. Sebastian, his flesh penetrated by arrows, which do not cause undue pain or suffering because he understands the nature of his wounding—an understanding which in the case of the analyst is the product of his or her own analytical experience and training analysis. The healing comes through the consciousness of one's own authentically lived life.

In dealing with eating disorders, it is imperative to separate the symptom from the disease. The symptom may be obesity, loss of weight, and/or vomiting. The analysand usually wants to correct "the weight problem." Weight in itself, however, is not necessarily a problem, although current collective attitudes would lead one to believe that success or failure in life and love depends on whether one is fat or thin. Some people by nature carry more weight than others; their big bodies radiate energy and are the right carriers for their psychic dimensions. If through illness or dieting they become thin, they are diminished. Others carry extra weight to counterbalance a highly intuitive, imaginative nature that tends to slip out of its physical home; it therefore needs the extra weight until it finds its grounding in its own earth. Weight gains and losses can vary within a wide range without any change in caloric intake if, for instance, such a person is engaged in artistic creation or is closely relating to someone who is dying. The disease is not the weight, but rather the psychological wounding that is manifesting through the eating disorder. The analyst through her body responses can recognize whether the body sitting opposite is a mound of unconscious flesh or whether it is a conscious body, and, by watching its fluctuation in weight, she can keep a very conscious eye on shadow activity. The process, as I see it in working with eating disorders, is to recognize the wounded instincts, to nurture and discipline them back to health, and to bring the ego into a loving, firm relationship to them. Then the body gradually and naturally becomes the right container, whether large or small or fluctuating, for that particular psyche.

This cannot happen if the analyst is consciously or unconsciously measuring the analysand's progress by watching her weight—and in this paper I use the feminine possessive throughout as all these analysands are female. In most cases, the patient has spent years losing or gaining a few hundred pounds before coming to analysis as a last resort. Her home environment has encouraged a rigid life style, controlled by the clock, examinations, and professional goals. She has attempted to diet by reinforcing these rigid patterns through strict adherence to caloric charts and routine exercises. The real needs of her starving shadow and starving ego have been ignored. The psyche has ultimately rebelled and the rejected instincts have erupted in compulsive eating behavior. To try to deal with that frenzy directly is to face Medusa head on, and, inevitably, Medusa will win. If, on the other hand, psyche and soma are recognized as one interrelated system, the dreams will quite clearly point out when the ego is strong enough to deal with the inferior function. The analyst merely by remaining conscious of the physical proportions in the opposite chair is holding the necessary tension. If that tension is lost, then the unconscious conflict manifesting in the body is forgotten; analyst and analysand are probably flying with golden intuitive dreams, unaware of the abandoned shadow that is too deeply buried even to appear in dreams.

One illustration will make the process clear. Rachel is in her early thirties, the daughter of an extremely rational father and equally intuitive, artistic mother who expected her daughter to be as "charming" as she, which, unfortunately, she was not. The mother's message had long been, "The chocolate cake is in the kitchen. Don't eat it." Rachel's logic is constantly at war with her intuition. Her dream is to walk into a bookstore and find a book, *The Answer,* by God. Since childhood she has been a rebel against the affluent society into which she was born, a rebellion which has manifested itself in, among other things, drug and food abuse. Her terror of deprivation made dieting impossible. After two years of analysis she had the following dream:

Dream: *Thor ran out into the street chasing two other black dogs. They went round a bend and caused a car crash. I had to talk to the policeman.*

*"Don't make me put him down," I said. "He is in train-
ing."*
"Okay," the policeman replied.

After that dream her craving for sweets stopped. Her beloved
dog was in fact in training because he acted out her hostility and
nipped people. Disciplining him under the tutelage of an excellent
trainer, she became aware of her own "uncivilized" instincts and
the chaos they created in her body. She also became conscious of
how rejected she felt because she was "unsuitable" by collective
standards. On one level her size isolated her even from her friends.
Indeed, she was receiving a double message: "We love you but we
don't accept you the way you are."

Two weeks later, a friend gave her home baked brownies. "I
must have chocolate," she thought and ate six brownies. Earlier this
would have been standard behavior; now she was ill. That night she
dreamed:

Dream: *Went with friends to the Bahamas. They had made an
inexpensive deal because it was an island army base surround-
ed by buzzing war planes.*
*"You can always get cheaper holidays by going to army
camps," they said.*
"Never again," I thought. "No bargain. I don't like it here."
*I was going to go to Paradise Island with one friend. Then
it switched and I was going with my brother to see my mother.
She was dying and I had to see her twice before she died. She
was lying on the couch she had had when I was a kid, bandages
on her eyes. There was something evil about her, like Cathy in*
East of Eden. *She was Evil. She looked at me with that "something is wrong with this relationship" look. It's her way of
looking; she is going to see the sordid underside of everything.
She asks about my trip. I knew she wanted to see sordidness in
it, so I said, "People make up rumors." I wouldn't let her in.*

The "inexpensive deal" on the island army base probably sym-
bolizes Rachel's undifferentiated autonomous complex, an area
where she anticipates freedom from responsibility, but in fact confronts buzzing hostile intuitions. As long as she puts cheap energy
into the complex, she is going to be preparing for war. The dream
ego decides it is no bargain and leaves for yet another Paradise.
However, the dream shifts, and she and her animus go to her

unconscious mother. "Chocolate," she said, "brings back mother and her double messages in a big way." That confrontation with Evil made her ill, so ill that sweets became poison to her. "I never decided to diet," she said. "I won't diet, but I won't eat poison either." Thus the instincts, if given a chance, eventually become the friendly animal who will support the ego against the self-destructive component in the maternal unconscious.

The rejected child in the shadow, the child who would escape to Paradise Island, is the crucial figure in transference/countertransference in dealing with a food addict. Clothed in a persona that seems to reveal self-control, self-confidence, even a certain taciturn aloofness, the immature ego is constantly threatened by the witch child shadow who is terrified of deprivation by the witch mother. However loving the actual mother may have been, if the essence of the actual child was denigrated or ignored and the projections of "best little girl, best little student, best little athlete" accepted, then the unlived life is starving in the shadow. It does not believe that there will always be food or love. Its experience has taught it to take whatever sweetness is available right now because it will surely disappear. The buoyant animal energy that reached out for recognition during infancy has been "corrected" and caged until it no longer recognizes its own fear, guilt, and rage. The addict only knows that her life is intolerable and the only way to survive is to deaden the pain of the inner volcano by swallowing food or concentrating on not swallowing it. If the pressure of the volcano has to be released, then she may resort to ritual vomiting. Because she cannot live her own life in reality, she lives alone in her own imagination where she is queen. There she has her own private jokes, her own bitterness against the world that rejects her, which she in turn rejects. She creates her own moral values and does not hesitate to lie or steal in order to feed herself what she wants and needs. In fact, almost every morsel she puts in her mouth is "forbidden fruit" and eaten with surreptitious glee in mocking defiance of the collective, "Thou shalt not." She is charged with blocked energy which she "knows" would destroy "ordinary" peole if it were unleashed; she concretizes her powerful feelings in her body, fearful of rejection if she lets them flow. Often that child is indeed supersensitive, highly intuitive, quick to recognize that others project their own witch child onto her because she is fat and fat is taboo in our culture. Often she is the abandoned one, left for dead in a schizophrenic society that loves her rational mind, exploits her sensitive soul, and rejects her powerful body. She does not want to be seen in sessions any more than she wants to be seen in life, and her smoke screen of silence and lies is impressive.

Yet that infantile, stubborn, treacherous shadow often contains the real feminine ego that has never had a chance to live. She looks to me for the understanding she no longer hopes to find in society. She is willing to allow me to hold the mirror up to her illusions and her lies. Together we can call a spade a spade. Fat is fat, greed is greed, lust is lust, power is power, love is love. I think of myself as a tuning fork which must ring true if it is to resonate with her reality. In a life and death struggle (in anorexia nervosa, for example) there is no time for euphemisms.

In situations where repressed rage and despair have led to eating and starving compulsions of demonic intensity, the patient appears "possessed." The terrorized ego then looks to the analyst for a lifeline. If the analyst fails to recognize the "loss of soul" involved in euphoric bingeing and starvation, or if the analyst is afraid of death, then the rigid body in the other chair may be dismissed as a self-dramatizing hysteric, prone to negative inflation and playing yet another trick to attract the attention of the analyst. The body rigidity, however, may be caused by inundation of the ego by overpowering emotions, as in the catatonic state of schizophrenics. The analysand may be close to a psychotic episode. A life and death struggle may be going on which needs to be dealt with at that level if depth healing is to take place. The obsessive emotions need the shield of the analyst's consciousness to reflect what is constellated. That reflection can drive out the possession and release the petrified emotions. To cope with this, the analyst needs to know her own strength in dealing with or choosing not to deal with the archetype of evil. If the analysand's weak ego is committed to beauty, light, and truth, it is vulnerable to invasion by the dark aspect of the Self, and the analyst may suddenly find herself turned to stone. Speaking of evil, Jung says,

> . . . it is quite within the bounds of possibility for a man to recognize the relative evil of his nature, but it is a rare and shattering experience for him to gaze into the face of absolute evil. (1959, par. 19)

The spirit who would lure a woman to her death is something darker than part of the personal shadow. When the analysand has not sufficient animus development to defend against that constellation, the analyst takes on the role of Perseus, the positive animus. In some cases, however, depth analysis is out of the question. The most that can be achieved is a sealing off of the witch's cauldron. An analysand can at least be helped to recognize that she need not play the fool and walk in where angels fear to tread.

In this short paper it is not possible to develop the various stages of transference/countertransference. A general pattern must suffice. Usually the obese, anorexic, or bulimic patient has acted as a buffer in an overly close-knit family. As a result, she lacks ego boundaries, physically and psychically. She also lacks close body-bonding with her mother and, therefore, with her own body. She may not appear in her own dreams. She is fearful of having anyone invade her precarious space. During the early stages, the analyst usually carries the transference of the Self, even to the point of answering such a seemingly innocent question as "What will you be eating this week-end?" Generally, the analysand has carried and is carrying a projected, idealized image from one or both parents, but one or both have turned against her internally, and what was once an admiring audience has become an introjected, annihilating judge. Fearful of losing the love of the analyst as well, the analysand will not express her true self. Rather she reveals the idealized, projected image with which she has always lived. The analyst, acting as mirror, reflects that image, only obliquely suggesting the compensating shadow sides. Gradually, the analysand can believe that she will not be rejected if she does reveal who she in fact is; gradually her right hand begins to acknowledge what her left hand is doing.

While the analyst may be acting as both father and mother in the beginning of the analysis, the next stage, if the analyst is a woman, is usually to become a medium for the archetype of the Great Mother, she who re-mothers without the original conflict, the mother who is accepting, somewhat directive, loving, and non-judgmental. Often a very powerful dream of the Great Mother shakes the analysand's rational roots. "I don't know what's going on," she will say. "I'm not a religious person, but now I have this inner sense of peace. I know somebody up there loves me." During this phase, the analysand can be brought to deal with her eating disorders by trying to incorporate Good Mother into herself: nourish herself with good food, love her body, cherish herself as a woman in a way which her mother was unable to do. Former rigid patterns of behavior and attitudes can be replaced by trust and hope, and relaxation into the body's musculature and into the ground of reality. Dreams of birth and little girls quickly growing from one year to puberty appear in this stage.

Grounding in the instincts is crucial. "What do I need to nourish myself? Am I hungry? Will this food satisfy my hunger or is it another kind of hunger? What colors do I like? Do I receive any messages from my body? What is it trying to tell me? Am I angry? Am I frightened? When am I using food to swallow down my feelings? What other types of food would feed my soul? How do I relate to other women? What is this new energy flowing through me?" During this stage, I accept the role of mother to my growing daughter, being firm and loving, encouraging and practical, especially in the details of everyday living. Essentially this is the process in any analysis in which the analysand is not rooted in the body and is without a strong ego structure. The difference with eating disorders lies in the intensity of the conflict. The stakes may be high and immediate.

Last year, for example, I was working with a 33-year-old woman who seemed to have progressed very well during two years of analysis. She had had an eating disorder earlier in her life, but that seemed to have been solved, and so we focused on building her ego. Although she had a highly developed masculine side, and a finely developed intelligence, and although she had a professional position which required all her capacities for leadership and initiative, her feminine side was quite infantile. Her capacity to objectify her own pain deceived me into believing she was more mature than in fact she was. I believed she had a good understanding of a vicious negative mother complex, and together we could laugh at some of the extraordinary images her unconscious would present. After two years of slowly building up trust together, we had what seemed to me to be the best session to date. I had been very straight with her in speaking about her dream ego and said, "You are your mother's daughter." I sensed that that comment had not been accepted, but felt she was strong enough to deal with it or throw it back at me. What I had not taken into consideration was the "solved" eating disorder and the fact that she had been on a fruit fast for almost a month.

That night she had a chaotic dream, part of which was as follows:

Dream: *Out of nowhere a young man comes over to us. He wants to choke me and to kill me. I'm terrified. He is possessed*

by the Devil. It's not a young man after all. It is Marion [the
analyst]. She's raging at me, choking me, killing me. She pulls
back. She is vomiting over me, green bile. I'm terrified, held
motionless by my fear. I must get away from her, save myself.
Marion has pulled away from me. She continues to vomit, to
come at me again and again. There is a horrible screaming in
the air. I manage to lift myself from the chair. I back slowly and
motionlessly away. I manage to wake from this horror.

   My body is drenched; the sheets are torn from the bed. I'm
clinging to the back of the bed, frozen. My head, my ears are
ringing, a raging ring, church bells sounding mass. My eyes
search the room to see if Marion has really left. Real terror
overcomes my whole body.

   I got to work that morning; I don't know how. Half an hour
into my work I ran to the washroom to vomit.

Fortunately, the analysand phoned. She came into the office in
a "loss of soul" state. A severe enantiodromia had taken place. At
the very point of what seemed genuine trust between us, the good
mother flipped into the negative witch, flipped because of my one
premature remark, my misjudging of her psychological maturity and
her weakened physical and psychic condition. (Food deprivation,
as the mystics know, can evoke archetypal dreams, confrontations
with Good or Evil.) At this point the analysand felt herself in danger
of throwing herself off her balcony. This analysis really began at this
point, however, because the analysand had the courage to stay with
me and with her dreams, and after four weeks the "possession"
passed, and we both settled into working with the clearer picture of
her unconscious situation.

Another distinguishing factor in dealing with eating disorders
is the body in the other chair. The analyst who is sitting opposite
250 pounds of blocked energy in one hour, and opposite 90 pounds
of skin and bone in the next, needs to know exactly what unconscious responses are being evoked in the analyst's own body. The
analysand is poised for the slightest sign of rejection—conscious or
unconscious. Analysts, like everyone else, are the products of a
culture that worships the great goddess Thinness, and we have to
be careful of our own shadow response to 250 pounds in the other
chair. We cannot constellate the analysand's inner healer if we
unconsciously reject her size. She and her body are enemies as it is,
and our unconscious projection can rend the hostile sisters even

further apart. At some point the analyst who has unconsciously rejected the abandoned body will become the target for the pent-up rage that will erupt against her, because the old game is still being played out—the old game of let's pretend "the ugly one" is not here. She has done the same thing to herself by refusing to step onto a scale, by refusing to look into a mirror, by refusing to buy clothes or enter a crowded theatre. If the analyst off-handedly asks in each session how her clothes are fitting, what movie she has seen, what airplane trip she is planning, she begins to think of herself as a member of society. Fat is fact and the body must be accepted and dealt with. Otherwise, at some point, the transference/countertransference will be demolished by the rejected demon—the demon who hates God, the demon who has ostracized her from a world into which she never wanted to be born anyway, a world in which she is sick of trying to justify her existence, a world in which she feels her ugliness has no right to exist. The vampire who sucks her life blood has to spew out his vitriolic poison sometime, but he cannot shatter the container if the analyst genuinely believes that psyche and soma are one, that accepting her is accepting her body.

The demon may emerge when enough weight has been lost to bring up the problem of relationship to a man. Now the real problems of her femininity and her sexuality must be faced—problems that have been masked by the eating disorder. In many cases, the body, whether fat or bone, has acted as the glass coffin which sealed the girl-woman into her idealized father, thus sealing other men out. Now if a suitor appears, the demon is threatened. "You are mine," he hisses. "Get that man out." Repeatedly, suicidal fantasies emerge as soon as men begin to find her attractive, or she may regress into the obsession. Suddenly she is forced to recognize the idealized image that father and perhaps mother have projected onto her and the idealized image that she has projected back. She is trapped in an inflation which would make her an impenetrable goddess, and men either gods or rapists. If she rejects what her parents projected onto her, guilt entraps her. However, if the weight loss is to be maintained and continued, she has to recognize the inflation in order to exorcise the weight of the idealized projection and her identification with it. This involves surrendering her perfectionist ideals and accepting her own humanity[1]—and the humanity of the man she might love. This is unquestionably the most difficult

---

1. For a fuller discussion of this theme see Woodman (1982).

transition stage and needs to be worked at from the outset of the analysis; otherwise a weight gain or loss is inevitable. The despair of a lifetime surfaces—the recognition of her own unlived femininity. She often has to face her psychically incestuous relationship to her father and her hostile feelings toward her mother. She looks to the analyst for reassurance that she is acceptable, even if she is not perfect. Essentially, she is terrified to walk out of her cage and take responsibility for her own life.

This is a time of woman-to-woman bonding between analyst and analysand; lesbian dreams may appear. There is often a sense of mourning involved which the analyst may have to mirror in order to bring it to consciousness. The body in which the analysand has lived is no longer there to act as whipping post, or armor, or protective home in which she can be invisible. The woman can now recognize what a magnificent friend her body has been and how undeserving of her ruthless punishment. She will also have to own her cage, which she has projected onto other people. Conscious rituals are helpful in allowing the former body image—fat or thin— to disappear, leaving room for the new. A new consciousness of the body as the temple of the feminine soul prepares the way for mature sexuality—sexuality integrated with spirituality.

Women often come to me because they say they are afraid to go to a male analyst. "I know I will fall in love with him," they say. "I don't want that. I want to concentrate on my analysis." They know themselves well enough to know that their bonding with their father is so deep that any close spiritual relationship to a man can have only one outcome. These are often women with critical eating disorders because their life is in their spirit. If a girl has been her father's darling, bound to him in spiritual incest, she is doomed to transfer that love onto a male analyst. If she is a creative woman, her creativity is born out of that bonding. Her relationship to her body is negligible because her relationship to her mother is uncertain and her reality is in her imagination. Her archaic sexuality is in her unconscious body, so that while she may have many lovers, no man can conquer her through her sexuality. She may be a *femme fatale*, but she lives, moves, and has her being through the father or the father surrogate. Although her analysis may be incredibly productive, although her weight stabilizes, and although her life blossoms, once the transference/countertransference is broken, she has once again lost her soul. The analyst has become her trickster father, the complex that drove her into analysis in the first place. Of course, the analyst's pain may be every bit as great as hers. The crux of the situation, as I see it, is that the analyst has allowed the transference to take the place of creating an ego structure strong enough to contain the influx of wealth from the unconscious. To hold the tension between the opposites in such an analysand is a huge challenge. The analyst has to take a long look at his own countertransference and work with it creatively in order to allow the projections to be gradually withdrawn. Body work can be very valuable in the transition period because it gives her soul a home to come back to and to go out from.

Middle-aged women with eating disorders almost always recognize that their real problem is a spiritual one. "If it were right with God," they say, "it would be right with my body." Their children have left, their husbands may be engrossed in business, dead, or divorced, and their sense of despair seems bottomless. With them, as with younger women, it is very important to distinguish whether the eating disorder is lifelong or recent. A woman who has never found herself but who has survived because she is identified with the role of mother and wife may suddenly collapse into the despair which has been dormant for years. She looks to the analyst to save her. The analyst can only strive to develop her commitment to her own dreams and inner life. While the sessions may be sustaining, any transformation comes about only when the analysand accepts responsibility for her own destiny.

If the transference is ultimately the analysand's responsibility, the countertransference is ultimately the responsibility of the analyst. At each stage of growth the withdrawal of projections in the analysand is accomplished by corresponding withdrawals by the analyst. The inner letting-go allows the other to progress; the process is mutually shared. Through the transference and the dreams of the analysand, the analyst discovers unexplored territories in herself; through the countertransference, the analysand experiences herself from a totally new perspective. "The intersection of the timeless moment" (Eliot 1952) is the still point in which both receive healing.

In this paper I have placed greater emphasis upon countertransference than upon transference because I am increasingly realizing the creative role it can play in the healing process. The observer does influence whomever he or she is observing. If the analyst has genuinely confronted her own shadow and learned to love the enemy, then the stone which the builders rejected does become the cornerstone of the new building. Then countertransference may serve as a healing balm. In Christian terms, as well as Jungian terms, the love of the enemy is not natural, but *contra naturam,* not Eros but Agape. It is, as Jung described it, a form of grace arising from sacrifice, a resurrection coming out of death.

In playing the many roles assigned by the analysand—Self, Mother, Father, Demon Lover—the analyst must play them "with a difference." The essential difference is that they are not roles at all in some theatrical or fictional sense, but psychic realities from which the analysand is cut off. The fiction resides not in the analyst but in the analysand. The obese, the anorexic, and the bulimic do not believe that they are human because their humanity has been too long rejected. Life for them consists of role playing and one of their sole sources of comfort and compensation is their belief that "All the world's a stage/And all the men and women merely players"—a "phony" role which they disdainfully reject but at the same time despairingly yearn for. Repeatedly they assert that what applies to other people does not apply to them. As Elephant Men, they take refuge in some subliminal conviction that they are invisible, a conviction supported by the fact that people seldom meet them eye to eye or remark directly and honestly upon their appearance.

One day in our waiting room, one of my obese patients was waiting with two or three others, reading at the big table. She was so engrossed in her magazine that she failed to realize she was blocking my way into the next room.

"Good heavens, Louise, move your big fanny," I exclaimed. "Can't you see I can't get through?"

Silence dropped like a pall. The other analysands glared at me with shocked horror, and at her with compassionate curiosity. When Louise came in for her session, she was roaring with laughter, precariously close to sobbing.

"Did you see their faces," she laughed, "when they were forced to recognize me? For over a year I've been sitting invisibly in that room and when I was finally seen, nobody knew what to do with me. I was real."

Her sense of exhilaration, with its undercurrents of rage and despair, filled my office. It was as if she had made her first appearance in the world and I was the midwife announcing, "It's a girl!"

That is what I mean by making the stone the builders rejected into the cornerstone of the building. This is what I mean by creative countertransference. The others in the room could not deal with the piercing by the arrow—the wound of her flesh. They couldn't because they had never confronted it in themselves, or worse, were now in the process of confronting it and had yet to work it through. The obese, the anorexic, and the bulimic who are in the throes of their own pain can hardly endure the sight of an obese woman. To be able not only to endure it, but to love it for the psychic and spiritual journey it may evoke, is, I believe, the countertransference of a love that may assist in the healing process that has behind it and within it the energy of the Self.

References

Eliot, T. S. 1952. Four quartets. In *The complete poems and plays: 1909-1950*, p. 139. New York: Harcourt, Brace.

Jung, C. G. 1959. *Aion: Researches into the phenomenology of the self.* In *Collected works*, vol. 9, part 2. Princeton: Princeton University Press.

Woodman, M. 1982. *Addiction to perfection: The still unravished bride.* Toronto: Inner City Books.

Power, Shamanism, and Maieutics in the Countertransference

Murray Stein

Harriet Machtiger's (1982) provocative discussion of counter-transference in *Jungian Analysis* presses for a more candid literature from Jungian analysts on this crucial topic. She points to the "almost phobic response" of analysts to questions about "the revelation of what transpires in the countertransference or in the analysis itself" (1982, p. 93), a response that she interprets as a defense against critical self-examination.

The reason such a stunning lacuna exists in the psychological literature, I believe, is that countertransference has been and remains lodged in the shadow of analytic practice. Neither in the literature nor in analytic practice is this topic discussed extensively because analysts resist the analysis of it. It is too painful, too conflicted, and too much implicated in the analyst's own unwashed psyche. So these attitudes and reactions, which are deeply involved in the analytic process at every moment, are fended off and repressed.

Murray Stein, M. Div., is president of the Chicago Society of Jungian Analysts and has a private practice in Wilmette, Illinois. A graduate of Yale College, Yale Divinity School, and the C. G. Jung Institute of Zurich, he is the editor of *Jungian Analysis* (1982) and the author of *In MidLife* (1983).

This defense against disclosure of countertransference and against analysis of its sources has to be breached if we are to come close to understanding what happens in analysis, for better *or* worse. So I strongly support Machtiger's call for a more courageous discussion of countertransference. Perhaps this will force us to rethink the ways we use, fail to use, or misuse countertransference attitudes and reactions in analysis.

Our field does seem to have reached the point of agreeing that countertransference is inevitable in analysis and can be extremely useful for therapy if correctly understood and handled. Machtiger even asserts, "It is the analyst's reaction in the countertransference that is the essential therapeutic factor in analysis" (1982, p. 90), making the strong point that the necessary healing "reaction" is *interpretation*. Machtiger insists that countertransference must be interpreted in analysis:

> One of Jung's basic premises was that the patient's illness needs to be met by the analyst's health. This interaction requires the confrontation and conscious interpretation of the conscious and unconsious contertransference/transference position of both analyst and patient, and the subsequent integration of the contents. (p. 100)

By interpreting countertransference, therefore, the analyst is demonstrating basic health and modeling a way to work on transference.

As a discipline, however, analytical psychology is only starting to develop its thinking about countertransference, and consequently Jungian analysts often find it awkward and difficult to work with it in therapy. We still need to clarify the great sea of unconsciousness in which this factor of analytic work washes about; we also need to describe the stupefying variety of images, feelings, psychological dynamics, and structures involved in countertransference attitudes and reactions. While it is true that countertransference has been discussed occasionally by Jungian analysts from a theoretical perspective (as attested to by Machtiger's excellent review of the literature), the wide variety of its manifestations still remains largely undisclosed and uncataloged, let alone carefully analyzed or understood.

Is it really so important, though, for analysts to become aware of and to interpret the countertransference? Doesn't "healing" take place just as well without this uncomfortable labor? It is certainly true that many Jungian (and other) analyses end without a very thorough clarification of mutual projection and perception (Jung's *"Auseinandersetzung"*) between anayst and analysand, but it may be charged that these analyses are not completed either. For the transference cannot be resolved, much less integrated, unless the projections and counterprojections of analyst and analysand have been sorted out. We want analysands to walk away from analysis as whole and intact persons, so the ownership of these pieces of psyche and an understanding of how they interact with others need to be clarified. This is the aim of analysis when the transference/ countertransference process is being interpreted and raised to consciousness: The base of mutual unconsciousness from which it operated is brought to light and worked through.

We need to begin thinking of a "stage" or "phase" of analysis when this kind of interpretive work on the transference/counter-transference process is the primary focus. The "conscious interpretation of the conscious and unconscious countertransference/transference position of both analyst and patient" (Machtiger 1982, p. 100) must become a more central aspect of Jungian practice than it has been. It remains an unresolved (almost an undiscussed) question of technique *when* this should be done: early in analysis, late, or throughout?

A few basic discriminations regarding countertransference have been made in the analytic community. There is the easy conversational distinction between positive and negative countertransference, which mirrors the notion of positive and negative transference. This seems to say, basically, that an analyst "likes" the analysand or doesn't. As a point of reference this is not altogether useless or beside the point, but it leaves a lot to be desired in the way of detail.

A more interesting and analytically useful distinction has been made between countertransference that originates autonomously in the analyst's psyche (Fordham's [1978] "illusory," Dieckmann's [1976] "projective," Racker's [1968] "neurotic" countertransference) and countertransference that originates in response to the analysand's psyche (Fordham's "syntonic," Dieckmann's "objective," Racker's "concordant" countertransference). This distinction breaks down, however, because, as Machtiger points out, the two subjects involved in this relationship cannot be separated so neatly. It is impossible to tell with complete assurance who owns which psychic contents in the transference/countertransference process. Nor is it possible to be sure who is in a reactive state to whom, or to what: Is the analyst reacting to the analysand's unconscious, or activating it? And vice versa. Jung pointed out that in the complex process of transference/countertransference *both* analyst and analysand "find themselves in a relationship founded on mutual unconsciousness" (1946, par. 367), and both contribute unconscious impetus to it. I do not believe that *any* transference or countertransference is purely intrapsychic-active or purely interpersonal-reactive. Countertransferences are always *both* illusory and syntonic, at one and the same time. And yet these discriminations need to be made if we are ever to raise consciousness about the contents and dynamics of countertransference.

An added complication to the project of becoming aware of countertransference is methodological. The method commonly used heretofore by analysts, a combination of introspection and self-analysis, will not by itself discriminate "who owns which" bits of psychic material in transference/countertransference processes. Even if analysts choose consciously to examine their countertransference by use of this method, the task is still not within reach because the method is inadequate to it. By themselves, analysts are unlikely to get to the truth. All of the analyst's secret thoughts and fantasies can be exposed to light and still not reveal the actual countertransference, precisely because it *is* unconscious. So self-analysis and confession are not enough. A method that is up to the job of analyzing countertransference must possess the power to search out the analyst's unconscious, as well as conscious, attitudes and reactions.

That method might look to several sources for information. Analysands are highly sensitive (consciously or unconsciously) to countertransference, and they reveal it to their analysts either in fantasies and dreams or through associations and indirect communications. Their testimony could be a primary source of data. Second, analysts' unconscious reactions to analysands, as indicated in dreams and spontaneous fantasies and in associations to analysands' material, could be collected and examined. Finally, analysts' interventions in the actual setting of therapy could be carefully observed, since they are strong indicators of countertransference. If analysts gathered and analyzed these materials, they would come much closer to an accurate appraisal of countertransference than the older method could possibly achieve.

Need for Control Analysis

To carry out this method to the fullest extent, it would be necessary to submit one's work to close case supervision with an analyst who was intent on examining all of one's interventions, associations, and relevant dreams and fantasies as well as those of the analysand. By using this kind of rigorous control analysis, Jungian analysis as a field would come much closer to a detailed account of countertransference than it would by attempts to understand the phenomenon by conscious self-examination and confession.

Allusions and references to the three types of countertransference discussed here are scattered about in the Jungian literature, as the references indicate. While this delineation is not completely novel, it does add, I believe, detail and coherence to their portraits.

The names of the three types of countertransference I am discussing—power, shamanism, and maieutics—suggest their core values and dynamics as well as the kind of dyadic relationship they require. Each one produces its own characteristic images and anxieties and shows a distinctive, archetypally based patterning. For the analyst, each can function to discharge tensions and pressures that build up during analysis; each can also provide an (often partly unconscious) orientation for what he or she is doing; and each can release a satisfying stream of inner meaning and fulfillment when its requirements are met. They can all heal, but each can also create distortions and do harm. This is to say that none is all good, none all bad. Each needs to be analyzed when it appears to be getting in the way of therapy.

By no means do these three types cover the whole gamut of countertransference reactions. Countertransferences based on maternal-nurturant (cf. Machtiger 1982) and eros-sexual (cf. Schwartz-Salant, pp. 1–30 in this issue) patterns are more widely recognized and commonly discussed in the literature. The hope in naming these other three and reflecting on them is that this will help analysts to identify countertransference reactions and attitudes that are not maternal or sexual and will also encourage the description and discussion of still other types.

Power

In the course of analysis, the analyst will frequently feel strong or subtle pressure to take command of the situation and to wield power over the analysand. Power, by which I mean the need or desire to have control, is never absent from human relationships, and the therapeutic relationship between analyst and analysand is no exception. Evidences of this type of countertransference reaction are many: giving the analysand unsolicited advice about how to improve a mental attitude; recommending auxiliary types of therapy, medication, hospitalization; insisting on rigid compliance regarding time and place of treatment; making aggressive interpretations that establish dominance; trivializing other people's therapeutic effects on the analysand; terminating unilaterally. Every analyst knows the impulse to get and maintain control over analysands and over the analytic process, and most feel somewhat guilty about asserting power, at least blatantly, within the analytic context. Analysts are supposed to be without desire.

Analysands are not immune from the wish for power either. It is not unknown that analysands sometimes actually take control and assume the power position. When they succeed, the analyst's countertransference position may in turn rest on the relinquishment of power and the acceptance of helplessness. If this complete sacrifice of the wish to have power over the analysand and the analytic process sounds like an approximation to the ideal of the ascetic analyst, it may in fact be rooted in a counterwish to be controlled and led in a masochistic style.

The power issue is not solved by giving control to the analysand. Analysands will gradually become upset about their compulsive attacks on the analyst and about their need to keep control of the analytic process, and become anxious about their success in doing this, but the behavior will not stop until the need to control is analyzed. It cannot be analyzed, however, from the masochistic position: from there the analyst has no *analytic* power.

It is relatively useless to berate oneself or others for becoming involved in this type of transference/countertransference process, either on the one side of the power play or the other. More difficult, but analytically more helpful, is understanding why it happened and perceiving the dynamics that sustain it.

Guggenbühl-Craig (1971), the leading Jungian expositor of the power theme, holds that when the quest for power becomes paramount in the "helping situation," an archetypal unit has become split into two parts. I roughly designate these parts "the lesser" and "the greater": the ill patient versus the healthy doctor; the poor client versus the established, dominant social worker; the sinful penitent versus the holy confessor; the ignorant student versus the learned teacher, and so forth. (Or, vice versa: the healthy patient vs. the ill doctor, etc.) In analysis this same kind of thing may happen. An archetypal bipolar pattern gets split, the analysand accepting and carrying one side of it, the analyst the other. This takes place through mutual, usually unconscious, collaboration in which projection and projective identification are the key dynamics.

The effect of this splitting is emotional distance: analyst and analysand become very "different," and their relationship is colored by this feeling of "otherness." The analyst or the analysand (whoever is in the power position) seems transcendent from the process, affecting it Apollo-like from afar.

Naturally the analyst wants to know when and why this (or any other) kind of countertransference/transference process gets set up in analysis. It may be due to the analyst's original countertransference attitude, which is established and in place before a particular analysand ever walks into the office. It is simply a professional attitude, one of power and command. The analysand either accepts it and adapts, or rejects it and leaves. More often, though, the power dynamic becomes established as analysis proceeds, as the complexes of each partner become engaged with those of the other. Here the power pattern derives from the psychodynamics that operate between two specific individuals, while other areas of each person's life may remain realtively free of this pattern.

Certain personalities seek to bring out the sadist (or the masochist) in the analyst: They are unconsciously looking for someone to take charge and to assert power over them, to tell them what to do, to give them tough advice, to punish them for their inadequacy; or they are unconsciously driven to overcome and to dominate others. Analysts can be co-opted by these unconscious pushes and pulls to perform the relevant partnership role, identifying with one side of the split bipolar structure and projecting the other. The ensuing relationship enacts a psychodynamic that is internal to each partner but externalized and now shared between them. The cooperation, or collusion, of each partner is what needs to be analyzed and worked through.

When the power dynamic takes over in analysis, it is not usually very effective to say simply that an archetype has become split. The specific details of the transference/countertransference process that led to this point need to become conscious. What unconscious elements of both analysand and analyst played a part in this splitting? What belongs to whom? Both sides of the interaction need to be openly analyzed and worked through in the course of therapy.

In the dreams of female analysands who assume the masochistic position and offer a sadistic projection to the male analyst, for example, a sexual theme is often associated with this pattern. In the resulting transference/countertransference process an erotic relationship is enacted through the drama of domination and submission. Masochistic submission gains the bondage of love. Meanwhile the analyst finds himself unaccountably stimulated as he feels impelled to belabor the analysand about her shortcomings, to make excessively harsh or sarcastic interpretations, to belittle her achievements and attack her attempts at self-understanding, to criticize her for all of her failures in life. His countertransference reaction is partly syntonic and can therefore shed insight into the analysand's intrapsychic processes: In the countertransference he can feel the sadistic rage of the animus and directly experience the analysand's rejecting and punitive (usually early and parental) inner figures. This information can yield rich genetic and dynamic interpretations.

When this becomes a strong countertransference reaction and truly engages the personality of the analyst, it has an illusory side as well. When the analyst feels stuck and angry, unworthy of his fee, disinclined to go on with the analysand unless she begins snapping out of it and getting better, he is generally in the grips of this countertransference reaction and under threat of being overcome by his own internal self-attacks. The analyst is struggling to get control over his own chaotic unconscious, generally over a willful and unruly anima or mother factor that creates moods of inadequacy and self-denigration with respect to infantile components in the ego (shadow elements). He projects this infantile (shadow) image onto the female analysand and attacks her, or tries to shape her up, in the same way his internal mother or anima-sister attacks him and tries to make him grow up. The analysand is inflicted with the analyst's self-punishment and attempts at self-mastery.

While this countertransference reaction may be seen as deriving from a response to a specific analysand's unconscious, and legitimately interpreted as such, it is also derived from the analyst's own unresolved ego and anima problems and usually *not* also interpreted as such. Pulling out of the analytic process at this point would be the analyst's ultimate power play.

In analyzing the transference/countertransference process, both sides of the relationship need to be interpreted, the one in light of the other. In the complexity of this process, there are no *purely* individual or intrapsychic factors having no connecting synapses to the partner's personality. If the transference is analyzed without reference to the analyst's complex participation in it, analysands are likely to get the message that all the "sickness" is theirs. This will feed the masochistic position rather than offer any manner of insight into how that position triggers a sadistic attack or how as a strategy for achieving love it ends up in a loss of power. Without this insight, the pattern cannot be transformed because the underlying unconscious assumptions and splits are not brought to light in a therapeutically effective way. By analyzing the countertransference/transference process as a complex whole, on the other hand, the analysand can discover how this pattern operates and how it generates the interpersonal and intrapsychic stalemate that follows.

Whether one is analyzing the syntonic or the illusory aspects of a power countertransference, the job is not an easy one. But the two types present different problems. In the first, the countertransference is used to interpret the inner states of the analysand, and here it seems relatively easy to link countertransference to transference dynamics. In the case of an illusory countertransference, however, the analyst is called on to analyze projections upon the analysand, which have in turn produced complex discharge and emotional reactions in the analysand. The first type of analysis provides the analysand with insight into his or her intrapsychic, genetic, and interpersonal patterns; the second relieves the analysand of the burden of carrying the "healer's" projections.

Countertransference is never completely illusory, however, so the interpretation of it can always also be linked to transference. In the constellation of analyst-on-top power countertransferences, the analysand is in some sense unconsciously asking to be on the bottom and to be cured passively. So a countertransference/transference interpretation can be used to point to these features of the transference and to link them to the rage beneath the masochistic position, which the analysand feels about having to meet the world on *its* terms and having to engage life actively.

While it is important to recognize that power assertions—whether in the form of brow beating, advice giving, technique teaching, or pill pushing—never cured anyone of a deep psychological problem and have often done a lot of harm, it is equally essential to realize that sometimes the analyst's conscious assertion of power is exactly the correct and helpful thing to do. Power assertions for the sake of "holding" and for keeping an analysand to task are gestures of care and therapeutic concern. Generally an assertion of power is not well aimed when it comes from a chronic countertransference attitude or from a shadow response. It may work out quite well, however, when it is compensatory to an analyst's earlier too-passive approach that has gotten stuck. Here the impulse to take control and to get things moving can provide the force needed to interpret the earlier transference/countertransference process and to move beyond it.

A personal observation is that the power countertransference appears as a shadow aspect of analysts, particularly those who claim consciously to operate out of an "Eros model." In principle, of course, this makes sense, since power and love often form a pair of complementary opposites. Yet it is always a cause for wonder to see how glaring an unconscious power countertransference attitude can be without the "eros analyst" having the slightest inkling of it. Since this is genuinely of the shadow, these analysts are not able to discover it through conscious introspection or self-scrutiny, and the reactions of analysands only leave them puzzled. They are always surprised and nonplussed, and become exceedingly defensive when analysands or control analysts attempt to point it out to them.

One such analyst had a dream in which she was driving a powerful car and terrifying everyone in the vicinity by shooting a pistol out the window. She was not shooting directly at the people, however, but at an object off in another direction. Nevertheless the people were terrified, and the driver could not understand why they should be afraid of her; after all, she wasn't shooting at them, she was firing in another direction! If the analyst could have interpreted this dream, or could have accepted a control analyst's interpretation of it (which she unfortunately could not), she would have realized what was going wrong with so many of her patients: they were reacting to her unconscious power discharges, which were terrifying them, while her conscious intentions were not at all harmful or malicious. In fact, she was consciously committed to the idea of healing through love and intimate relationships.

Shamanism

In his written discussions of transference and countertransference Jung does not include much consideration of the power dynamic, although he does occasionally tilt his hat to Adler. But if he tends to gloss over the issue of power, he is equally inclined to emphasize a shamanic model of healing in the countertransference (cf., e.g., Jung 1921, par. 486; 1931, par. 163; McGuire and Hull 1977, p. 345). His numerous scattered remarks about transference/countertransference dynamics in analysis are cast largely in this mold: Analysts become infected by their analysands' illnesses and then effect a cure by healing themselves and administering the medicine they manufacture in themselves to the analysand via "influence." In analysis this shamanic healing process is, of course, carried out on a psychic rather than physical plane. As Jung depicts it, this is a very complex and subtle interaction, involving the whole personality of both partners in a kind of alchemical combination of psychic elements (cf. 1946).

If power dynamics create distance between analyst and analysand and a sharpened sense of their differences in value, the shamanic process yields the opposite result. Difference is smudged and distance collapsed in favor of psychological identification. Analyst and analysand experience each other as "sames" not as "opposites." As this process of psychological identification takes hold, the empathy flowing between the partners tends to intensify; what happens in the one also occurs in the other; they resonate psychologically to one another. And this is when the analyst becomes "infected." Psychic ailments like depression, anxiety, schizoid withdrawal, invasions of unconscious figures and impulses are experienced, often simultaneously, by the analyst as well as by the analysand because the two psychic systems run on parallel lines, the analyst's psyche bending to the features of the analysand's inner landscape. Through this kind of mirroring, the analyst's psyche absorbs and comes to reflect the analysand's "illness."

This type of countertransference, it might be imagined, occurs only with analysts who have excessively permeable ego boundaries and a sort of elastic sense of personal identity. But many analysts relax their ego defenses in therapy and open themselves to the other person's psyche, and psychotherapeutic training generally fosters their doing this to some extent. So this type of interactional process is not as rare as might be thought, particularly since these identifications often take place at a level that is deeply unconscious for both analyst and analysand, bypassing ego defenses altogether.

As a shamanic healer, however, the analyst not only becomes infected by the analysand's illness but also finds a way to cure it. As the illness is taken in and suffered, the analyst begins searching for a cure: analyzing the inner psychological constellation created by this illness; scrutinizing dreams, associations, and other unconscious material relevant to the suffering; looking for symbols that emerge from the unconscious and represent the healing factor at work; active imagination. The unconscious responds to the healer's suffering, and the analyst applies the curative symbols to the wound, thereby healing the illness. Out of a personal need for healing, then, the analyst has been forced to develop further by dealing with the effects created by the analysand's illness.

The therapeutic task now is to pass this *medicina* over to the analysand. Like catching the original infection, administering the medicine occurs by way of the countertransference/transference process: The analyst, Jung says, "influences" the analysand (1931, par. 169). Influence in this case implies not only the effects that can be achieved simply by giving good advice or recommending some healing rituals or even making acutely empathic interpretations, but it also embraces the notion that the unconscious is deeply involved in this interactional nexus. Analyst and analysand are bonded as much unconsciously as they are connected consciously, and it is through this channel, too, via the unconscious, that the *medicina* passes to the analysand. This is the meaning of the hackneyed observation that the "whole being" of the analyst is involved in the countertransference/transference process. The influence of the analyst's healing "substance" is carried to the analysand through many subtle capillaries that run between the two partners in this complex relationship.

In modern analytic terms, this shamanic cycle can be understood as a mixture of mutual *identification, projective identification,* and *introjection* between analyst and analysand. Analyst and analysand fall into a state of identification; they project psychic contents onto one another, and each identifies with these; each is introjected at some point by the other. (All of these dynamics were covered by Jung in the concept of *participation mystique.* Through *participation mystique,* which is largely unconscious, the analyst and analysand affect and are affected by each other.) The healing influence of the analyst's personality, which is constellated in response to the internalized illness of analysand, creates a curative effect within the analysand, because the analyst's self-healing process triggers a parallel healing process in the analysand's psyche. The analysand's own inner healing forces become activated by, or around, the healing analyst-imago.

This type of countertransference/transference process seems ideal in many ways for achieving the goal of psychological healing that many analysts seek. But shamanic wizardry in analysis is seductive and has its pitfalls. It can misfire and end in *folie à deux,* analytic stalemate, particularly when the dynamic sources of mutual identification go unanalyzed and remain unconscious. There is a strong temptation simply to fall into the flow of this process and to let it go on unanalyzed in the hope that it will create a magical cure. The shamanic process is not necessarily an ideal one, and analysts should be able to recognize it when it occurs, understand what it means and how it works, and foresee some of its dangers. For it creates many blind spots and can easily become anchored in the analyst's shadow, which in turn creates fierce resistance to analyzing this type of countertransference.

We saw that when power is the issue, opposites are split and a sense of sharp difference and opposition between analyst and analysand is constellated. The shamanic mode, on the other hand, is based on a constellation of identity between analyst and analysand. Here each psyche becomes oriented by an impulse to be as similar as possible to the other, with the result that each also becomes unconscious at the same points. Each shares, or tries to, the same psychological typology, the same level of maturity, the same masculine/feminine, ego/shadow constellations; even various inner objects—such as mother and father imagoes and complexes—become so thoroughly confused that the personal history of one can hardly be told from the other. Mutual idealization and denigration may occur, each person representing the other's alter ego or psychological "twin." The analyst's assumption that identity prevails in so many conscious and unconscious areas of course obscures analytic vision and enfeebles the "analytic grip." Analysis becomes a sort of self-analysis, with the same penchant for blindness to the shadow, and the real sickness and pathology are excluded from consciousness by mutual consent.

Shamanic countertransference, too, can easily veer toward becoming Fordham's (1978) "illusory" type. What the analyst is seeking to treat and to heal—a "bad mother" imago, for example—is actually being projected onto the analysand, who may comply by identifying with it and presenting it back to the analyst for treatment. The illusion is that the analysand is the source of the illness from which the analyst is suffering. Actually, the analyst's attempts at self-healing are not shamanic in this instance but simply efforts at self-healing, in which analysands act as receivers of projected unconscious material and as catalysts for self-therapy.

An ongoing shamanic countertransference/transference process can never be purely illusory, of course, because the analysand must have an internal capacity to accept the analyst's projection and to identify with it, which implies similar inner structures. But in the countertransference itself, as this transpires during therapeutic sessions, the analyst is striving for self-healing through working on what is identified as originally being the analysand's illness. (The analyst may feel better after these sessions, while the analysand feels worse.) Thus a reversal can occur by which the analysand becomes the shamanic healer, suffering in order to cure the analyst's illness. The transference-need to cure the analyst has been recognized (see Searles 1979), but the countertransference side of this, wherein the analyst unconsciously offers his illness to the analysand for shamanic treatment, has not been much remarked upon. This reversal of the therapeutic direction is the great unanalyzed shadow of the shamanic type of countertransference.

Maieutics

In his 1912 paper, *"Neue Bahnen der Psychologie"* ("New Paths in Psychology"), Jung used the term *maieutics* to characterize psychoanalysis:

> It is a catharsis of a special kind, something like the maieutics of Socrates, the "art of the midwife." It is only to be expected that for many people who have adopted a certain pose towards themselves, in which they violently believe, psychoanalysis is a veritable torture. For, in accordance with the old mystical saying, "Give up what thou hast, then shalt thou receive!" they are called upon to abandon all their cherished illusions in order that something deeper, fairer, and more embracing may arise within them. Only through the mystery of self-sacrifice can a man find himself anew. It is a genuine old wisdom that comes to light again in psychoanalytical treatment, and it is especially curious that this kind of psychic education should prove necessary in the heyday of our culture. In more than one respect it may be compared with the Socratic method, though it must be said that psychoanalysis penetrates to far greater depths. (par. 437)

Imaged in this statement is a type of countertransference: The analyst sits as midwife to a psychological birthing process, in which "something deeper, fairer and more embracing" than the former (persona-dominated) conscious attitude arises within the analysand. In this type of countertransference/transference relationship, analysts experience themselves as assistants to a creative process that is taking place within their analysands.

In this maieutic process, the central exchanges within the analytic relationship are seen as revolving around creativity and the revelation of the Self. Not mastery (power) or healing (shamanism) but birthing is the root metaphor for what is taking place. The analyst's task is to assist what is within the analysand's unconscious to reveal itself; then, receiving and accepting this "Self" into the world, the analyst facilitates its incorporation into the patterns of daily life.

In this countertransference, the analyst typically sinks into a state of deep receptivity to the analysand's unconscious; background becomes foreground and the unconscious becomes palpable. The analysand is meant to follow suit and also to become receptive to the unconscious, becoming self-maieutic to the unfolding drama of creativity and the Self's revelation. During times of struggle in this birth-giving, the analyst may want to attend to ego anxieties, but the basic commitment remains to a creative process that is appearing out of the invisible recesses of the unconscious. Often the analyst is captivated by a vision of the analysand's wholeness and futurity (the "child"), of a still largely unconscious Selfhood that must be brought to light and integrated. The analyst sees beyond the surface to the hidden core of a symptom's meaning. A divinity is perceived, a call heard for its recognition.

Jung's comparison of psychoanalysis to maieutics draws on the clinical experience of the differing images between what an analysand may hold consciously as a sense of Self at the beginning of analysis and the portrait of the Self that gradually emerges through a conscious exploration of the unconscious. The first is a persona-based false self, which has been constructed by a long process of identification and introjection; the second is the innate, antochthonous Self, which emerges in analysis as the unconscious is consulted and allowed to reveal its contents. As Jung points out in the passage quoted, a person's separation from a persona-based self and the recognition of another quite different image of the Self can be an extremely painful process. But it is one that can be ameliorated by the careful empathic holding of the maieutic analyst.

Analytic work is different of course from midwifery in many respects. One of them is that after midwives help to bring children into the world, their job is done, whereas analysis (like education) goes on and on. Unlike childbirth, the emergence of the Self is not a one-time event, numinous as a glimpse of it in a dream or waking vision may be. On the other hand, though, every analytic hour can be partly a maieutic event, in which an aspect of the unconscious Self is brought more into the light. Over a long period of time, many such mini-birthings add up to consciousness of the Self's vast complexity and richness. This conscious sense of wholeness is the "baby" whom the analyst hopes the analysand will carry away and take home at the end of analysis.

"Psychoanalysis, considered as a therapeutic technique," Jung writes, "consists in the main of numerous dream-analyses" (1912, par. 437). In the maieutic process, these have several key functions: to reveal where the "baby" is, at what stage of readiness for birth, how close to emerging into ego-consciousness, and also where the ego's defenses lie and where the tight spots of the passage to consciousness will be. Dreams function as X-rays, and the job of the "maieut" is to read them for information concerning the development of the process underway. Each dream interpretation is also, though, one of the many mini-births necessary to bring the Self up into the full light of day.

In the maieutic countertransference position, the analyst listens primarily for messages from the unconscious as they are spoken through dreams and through the noise of the ego's communications, often ignoring or discounting the ego's manifest meanings. The analysand, who too becomes involved in this maieutic process, may experience a gradual opening of the ego to the unconscious. Optimally he or she will develop feelings of profound trust in the capabilities of the analyst, who is fixed on penetrating beneath the surface to the unconscious core of meaning within the presented associations, images, words, and symptoms. The analyst is primarily focused on gathering together aspects of the unconscious Self—the complexes and archetypal images—and on glimpsing their internal unity and structure. This requires hearing and seeing through the play of words on the surface of conscious communication and taking sonarlike soundings of the depths beneath. Eventually a bit of truth about the analysand's unconscious Self comes clear and can be raised into consciousness.

While this countertransference position is based on a medical model of sorts—attending to the biological process of birthing—it is quite different from what we usually think of as such. The medical model normally implies clinical distance on the analyst's part, the image of a surgeon coolly detaching pathological tissue and afterwards leaving the patient to recover more or less on his own. In this surgical model the analyst hunts down pathology, attacks it, and tries to remove it from the analysand's personality ("remove the complex, clear up the distortions"). The maieutic attitude is very different: The analyst assumes a basically healthy process and is present to assist normal functioning. The sort of analysis that results from the maieutic stance may include some reductive analysis of ego defenses, even though an eye is kept all the while to the emerging self as it is growing and moving toward consciousness. The attitude of the analyst in the maieutic position is not purely passive and receptive, since there is an active role to be played in forcefully engaging defenses and resistances and sometimes in pushing through, or removing, them if they interfere with the birth.

The major pitfall in this countertransference attitude is that it may be illusory. The analyst may be gripped by a vision of the unconscious Self that is more his or her own than the analysand's. Birthing efforts are therefore unconsciously governed by a personal need to be creative and to give birth to a still unconscious Self. In this event, the analyst is projecting a creative process into the analysand, expecting to find a baby where there may even be no pregnancy, or, if so, only a false one.

In a sense, of course, it is always partly the case that analysis is maieutic for the analyst too. Through its action, and especially through the analysis of the countertransference, the analyst becomes more conscious of the Self that is forever somewhat unconscious. The analyst is also always still in the process of piecing together a greater awareness of the Self.

But it can happen that a chronic maieutic type of countertransference attitude occludes the analyst's vision. It may be intolerable for someone who operates habitually out of this attitude to realize that the unconscious of an analysand is not always pregnant and abundantly creative, and that some analysands are so riddled with ego deficits and encased in pathological defenses that pregnancy and giving birth are out of the question until these issues are resolved. It may well be that the analysand's ego is the infant that needs careful attention and holding rather than a still-to-be-born Self. The analysand for whom this is the case may attempt to comply with the analyst's expectations by producing something that looks like psychic pregnancy and new birth, but which is really play acting and adaptation to the analyst's expectation and never addresses the real person. A *puer aeternus* can produce one false rebirth experience after another, none of which moves the psyche ahead one inch. In a maieutic countertransference, the analyst can unconsciously collude with this resistance to analysis.

The analysis of this countertransference/transference process is no less tedious and repellent for the analyst than that of the others I have discussed. Examining one's own illusory and projective in-volvement in it is not an enviable task. It is particularly difficult when the countertransference lies primarily in the shadow of the analyst's conscious therapeutic stance. Consciously an analyst may support that he or she is working from a neutral objective attitude, for example, while unconsciously operating from a maieutic coun-tertransference. This unconscious attitude will exert pressure on the analysand to conform to type: If the analyst is going to be maieutic, the analysand must be, or rapidly become, pregnant. This uncon-scious message is communicated in many ways, among them through the interpretation of dreams, associations, and images. When the analyst is intent on birthing, the analysand had better come up with a fetus.

Analyzing this countertransference/transference process is no less important than analyzing the other types. Indeed this phase of analysis may be the only means by which a therapeutic process that has gotten stuck in this impasse can be freed for a more honest and exact analysis. Once the pressure to be pregnant and creative has been removed, the analysand can afford to be conflicted and sterile, if that is indeed the true psychological picture. The analyst is then able to see, accept, and work with a real person. When the maieutic countertransference is analyzed and put aside, the analysand is free to be whatever he or she is, and if pregnancy is in the cards, a true birth can take place in its own time.

Unless the analyst is utterly delusional, however, the maieutic countertransference is never altogether illusory. The analyst is at least partly responding to something in the analysand of which the analysand may not yet be aware. The constellation of the maieutic countertransference, therefore, may be an early sign of psychic pregnancy, a bit of clinical evidence that the Self is approaching. When it is syntonic, this countertransference response informs the analyst that the infantile aspects and future potential of the analy-sand's psyche are approaching and will soon reveal themselves. These will require empathic holding and containment, another maieutic function. So the stimulation of this countertransference as a reaction can be a harbinger of things that are still hidden in the womb of time and gestating silently in the unconscious.

The interactional approaches of Langs (1978) and of Goodheart (1980), it seems to me, are in many ways maieutic and reliant on the maieutic countertransference position. As such they are also liable to the pitfalls of this position. The analyst attends primarily to unconscious communications, to latent meanings rather than to manifest content. The "listening process" is tuned to the unconscious, ultimately to the Self. The analyst gathers these meanings and unconscious messages together and raises them to consciousness through interpretive comments. Goodheart's "secured symbolizing field," which implies reliable empathic "holding" on the analyst's part, is basically what I have in mind as a maieutic countertransference/transference process.

Theoretical Postscript

The unclarity of the discussion of countertransference—whether this term indicates all of the analyst's reactions to an analysand or only the more unconscious, complex-determined ones—could be resolved in part, it seems to me, by distinguishing between countertransference *attitudes, phases,* and *reactions.* By a countertransference attitude I mean an enduring, persistent set of conscious and unconscious images, values, and thought patterns, a psychological structure that continues through long periods of time and is present before, during, and after a particular analysis. Countertransference reactions, on the other hand, are temporary and fleeting, chiefly rooted in unconscious complexes and not under ego control, disruptive of the countertransference attitude. Countertransference phases are longer lasting than reactions, but they are contained within the overall structure of the countertransference attitude, often lasting throughout a phase of the analysis itself.

Each of these is made up of elements that derive from an analyst's psychological history. The countertransference attitude has roots in childhood, because an analyst will instinctively care for others as he or she was cared for originally. The analyst's psychological typology as well is a piece of this attitude. The countertransference attitude is also rooted in an archetypal core, whose specific nature (mother, father, hero, etc.) depends on the personal complexes in which the attitude is set. In addition to parental and archetypal figures, introjects of personal analysts and control analysts hold key positions in the makeup of the countertransference attitude: One treats others analytically as one was treated oneself. (Where parental and later analytic inner figures clash, a fundamental rift exists in the countertransference attitude, which creates an axis of vacillation that often disturbs the analyst and will frequently be observed and challenged by analysands who are particularly sensitive to nuances of relationship.) The same can be said about the elements making up countertransference phases and reactions: They too are rooted in the analyst's history, only they do not constitute the usual state of (professional) consciousness.

The specific elements that go into making up the countertransference attitude form the special features of an individual analyst's style of working and relating to analysands. Through training and experience, this attitude is adjusted, sharpened, made more conscious, but probably not changed fundamentally. The countertransference attitude is a more or less constant presence throughout analysis, a relatively stable factor among all the analyses an individual analyst conducts. This is the analyst's "face," so to speak.

A countertransference reaction, on the other hand, is more limited, extending through a few minutes of a session or through a few sessions, or limited to the analysis of particular kinds of persons. A reaction is distinct from the countertransference attitude, which it disrupts. It is a grimace on the analytic face. Whether syntonic or illusory, it is reactive to the transference, and it is usually derived from a fairly limited area of the analyst's unconscious. It can generally be dissolved by analysis.

A countertransference phase, in contrast to a reaction, stays within the structures of the more pervasive and enduring countertransference attitude and does not disrupt it. In a particular analysis, there are often periods when the analyst's attitude shifts subtly and, without being broken or disrupted, is augmented by a new attitude. A phase may perseverate for some sessions or even months, but one would not be inclined to say that the analyst had changed the basic countertransference attitude, only that some elements within it had been augmented, rearranged, or displaced. Like the more fleeting reaction, the phase is a reactive product within the analyst to the analysand's transference.

Each of the three types of countertransference discussed in this paper could, in a particular instance, be an attitude, a reaction, or a phase. Each type can constitute the relatively stable substructure on which the entire analytic practice rests; each can appear as a temporary countertransference reaction that disrupts the analyst's usual attitude; or each can form a phase within the context of another type of countertransference attitude. If we follow Jung's (1961, p. 133) insight on countertransference reactions, they are often products of unconscious compensation, which occur chiefly to modify an analyst's one-sided or distorted attitude toward a particular analysand.

The psychological dynamics operating within the analyst in transference/countertransference processes are different for countertransference attitudes, reactions, and phases. For useful analysis, the analyst should know what his or her countertransference attitude is, and what is a reactive, possibly a compensatory, departure from it. The main objective of control supervision, it seems to me, is to analyze the features of the countertransference attitude and to become familiar with the most frequently constellated types of countertransference reaction and phase. These insights will be of great value for the analysis of countertransference/transference processes in the course of the analyst's subsequent therapeutic work.

References

Dieckmann, H. 1976. Transference and countertransference: Results of a Berlin research group. *Journal of Analytical Psychology* 21/1:25–36.

Fordham, M. 1978. *Jungian psychotherapy.* New York: Wiley.

Goodheart, W. 1980. Theory of analytic interaction. *The San Francisco Jung Institute Library Journal* 1/4:2–39.

Guggenbühl-Craig, A. 1971. *Power in the helping professions.* New York: Spring Publications.

Jung, C. G. 1912. New paths in psychology. In *Collected works,* 7:245–68. Princeton: Princeton University Press, 1966.

_____. 1921. *Psychological types.* In *Collected works,* vol. 6. Princeton: Princeton University Press,1971.

_____. 1931. Problems of modern psychotherapy. In *Collected works,* 16:53–75. Princeton: Princeton University Press, 1966.

_____. 1946. The psychology of the transference. In *Collected works,* 16:163–323. Princeton: Princeton University Press, 1966.

_____. 1961. *Memories, dreams, reflections.* New York: Random House.

Langs, R. 1978. *The listening process.* New York: Jason Aronson.

Machtiger, H. 1982. Countertransference/transference. In *Jungian analysis,* M. Stein, ed., pp. 86–110. La Salle, Ill., and London: Open Court.

McGuire, W., and Hull, R. F. C., eds. 1977. *C. G. Jung speaking.* Princeton: Princeton University Press.

Racker, H. 1968. *Transference and countertransference.* New York: International Universities Press.

Searles, H. 1979. The patient as therapist to his analyst. In *Countertransference and related subjects,* pp. 380–459. New York: International Universities Press.

Successful and Unsuccessful Interventions in Jungian Analysis: The Construction and Destruction of the Spellbinding Circle

William B. Goodheart

The Clinical Sequence

A male therapist is seeing a new patient, and the therapist has recently decided not to allow smoking in his office, having even put his ashtrays into a drawer. The patient is an aggressive, 50-year-old, forceful man, who upon sitting down appeared anxious and wanted to know what to do. The therapist suggested that he begin wherever he liked and with whatever came to his mind; that things seem to work best that way. The patient spoke cursorily in sparse and concrete terms for the first few minutes about his having been shaky and anxious over the past year, about having developed an ulcer, and about having been in a hospital for a short time recently, altogether evincing general anxiety and moderate depressive and psychosomatic symptoms.

William B. Goodheart, Jr., M.D., is a member of the San Francisco Society of Jungian Analysts. A graduate of Stanford University, Stanford University School of Medicine, and the C.G. Jung Institute of San Francisco, he is assistant clinical professor of psychiatry at the University of California School of Medicine in San Francisco. He is president of the Society for Psychoanalytic Psychotherapy, Bay Area Chapter, an editor of the *International Journal of Psycholanalytic Therapy,* and an editor of *The Yearbook for the Society for Psychoanalytic Psychotherapy.*

The patient then asked the therapist to explain to him what he saw as the problem and what he ought to do about it. The therapist felt a bit pressured by this request so early on in their relationship. He became anxious and encouraged the patient to continue saying whatever came to his mind.

The patient then spoke about how perplexing these symptoms were since everything in his life was going fairly well. He had a successful business, a good sense about his wife, one son in college and another out working well at a job. He couldn't understand why he felt as he did.

There was another tense silence. The anxiety in the room grew into an atmosphere of high and severe tension. Suddenly the patient asked if he could smoke. The therapist responded, "Oh, do you want to smoke?" and found himself reaching over and anxiously, almost automatically, taking an ashtray out of the drawer and giving it to the patient.

The patient lit up a cigarette, inhaled, breathed a huge sigh of relief and began talking a bit more fluently for a short while. He spoke of his frequent travels, but that he didn't trust leaving his business in the hands of his partners since they didn't seem to have the ability to make solid decisions and they often seemed to get anxious at critical times. He wasn't sure of them. He hadn't liked being ill. . . . He didn't quite know what was going on. The doctors wanted to give him Valium, but he really didn't like going that route. But maybe there was something like a medicine that would help him. . . . He really had to get this under control fast, as it was interfering with his business. In fact, he wanted to get this cleared up to some degree by the start of the following week, because that was to be an important week. What does the therapist think is going on and could the therapist help him now or suggest something?

Two Psychic Systems in Reciprocal Interaction

As I approached this particular therapy sequence and tried to understand what was occurring between the therapist and his patient, I followed Jung's oft-repeated maxim that therapy is a dialectical reciprocal interaction in which two psychic systems enter together in what might be seen as a chemical or alchemical combination (see, e.g., 1966a, pars. 1, 8, 10, 163, 353, 354). This says to me that nothing happens in a therapeutic hour within the patient or the therapist which is not an interactional product. Another way of saying this is that the patient's behavior and communications throughout therapy are both a mutual product or amalgam of both the patient's intrapsychic life and an adaptive response to the interventions of the therapist. Consequently, the path to understanding the patient's intrapsychic life begins first with the comprehension of the sequence and flow of the specific interpersonal determinants and stimuli from the therapist to which the intrapsychic life of the patient is forming perceptions and imagoes, reacting, and adapting. From the beginning Jung emphasized that complexes are activated by stimuli, such as the triggering words in the word association experiments. Thus the actions of the therapist, both conscious and unconscious, are a stimulus towards the specific constellations of complexes in the patient and are a critical ingredient in the mutual product—the chemical reaction—which makes up each moment of therapy. The ongoing course of therapy is then a collection of such moments and is thus a mutual bipersonal production of action and reaction, of stimulus and response, between patient and therapist.

Following this metaphor of Jung's, I approach each hour of supervising or overlooking a therapy undertaking with as much interest in what the therapist says and does as in what the patient will say and do. In the clinical sequence just described, the therapist agreed to see the patient and to provide the unique space and opportunity for the patient to begin the process of self-exploration and therapy by putting his inchoate feelings and experiences into some sort of image and language of meaning. The patient's response was to sketchily mention his symptoms and then to become anxious and ask for concrete explanations and advice from the therapist. He had been referred by his internist and probably had gotten transient relief from his neurotic anxieties in the presence of this doctor by asking for and getting some soothing and simplifying intellectualized explanation, opinion, or diagnosis, which might have worked for the moment, but had obviously had no long-lasting effects. So it might be that he wanted, or expected, similar contact with this therapist, i.e., through this somatic and intellectualized mode of communication. Would this therapist join him in this maneuver to wall off his unconscious and gain some transient relief? This is a critical moment in the process of interaction with a patient in many ways for each of us therapists when the patient seems to be insisting on nonsymbolic and reductive responses from us. How do we respond in such situations?

Union Through *Imaginatio* Versus Through "Aberrant Natural Union"

Because I believe, with Jung, that symbols alone heal, that is, that the transformation of *materia*—feelings, impulses, anxieties, the instinctive dimension of the archetypal spectrum—into spiritual or meaningful substance is the ultimate vehicle of psychic transformation and individuation, I offer a minimum of concrete or nonsymbolic communications to patients. I feel to do so is not to work symbolically or alchemically, but reductively. In this case, for example, both therapist and patient already are meeting at this moment the undifferentiated unconscious, the shadow, in the form of inchoate, inarticulate, raw anxiety. It is nearly overwhelming the patient and is starting to seep into the therapist. It is the "material" of their interactional field. This is the beginning of the alchemical process, and it is to be expected. Jung called this "the first meeting with oneself" and likened it to a "passing through the valley of the shadow" (1966a, par. 399). It is the *"prima materia . . . an initial psychic situation,* symbolized by such terms as . . . chaos, *massa confusa . . ."* (1959, par. 240). At such moments, says Jung, "the maximal degree of consciousness confronts the ego with its shadow, and individual psychic life with a collective psyche. These psychological terms . . . denote an almost unendurable conflict, a psychic strait whose terrors only he knows who has passed through it" (1970b, par. 313). This is an early moment of "*nigredo* melancholia, a 'black blacker than black,' . . . an affliction of the soul, confusion" (1970b, par. 741). In my understanding the various stages of alchemy are embodied in these anxious moments within the interactional process of psychotherapy, which intensely involve each participant.

Yet the danger of the therapist's becoming "infected" by the patient is great at such anxious and pressured moments. The ego of the therapist is also threatened with becoming itself " 'a seat of anxiety' " (1970a, par. 360), with a corresponding loss of the essential maximal degree of consciousness. A strong choice must be made at this point by the therapist, and that is "consciously deciding not to become its [the shadow's] victim" (1966a, par. 420). To withstand the anxiety and unconscious pulls at such moments, the therapist is required to make a conscious, strong, willful act that attempts to relate to and seek an integration of conscious and unconscious by means of the patient's imagery.

This rich, alchemical, and nearly poetical language is really offering this therapist some sound guidance toward helping the patient in these first moments. It is simply saying: "Do not yourself become overwhelmed by anxiety nor by the pressure being put upon you by the shadow forces of this patient and yourself, which are clamoring for something other than the analytical experience. Offer this patient the art of remaining conscious and standing in relationship to one's unconscious forces rather than being flooded by them. Resist the interpersonal pressures from the patient's unconscious to adopt a stance other than that of the alchemical therapist, the guardian of symbols."

What is being maintained here is that the anxiety represents the fact that the opposites of the shadow-unconsciousness of the patient and the ego consciousness of the therapist have been constellated. When the opposites are constellated, Jung recurrently states, there are powerful, natural, infantile, and regressive forces that emerge from within a part of the unconscious which seek and pressure to reunite these opposites immediately so as to relieve the distress. These are the forces of "physical incest," says Jung; and he states further that "the psychopathological problem of incest is the *aberrant, natural form of the union of opposites*" (emphasis added) (1970*b*, par. 108). This patient is being unconsciously driven from within to seal over the constellation of opposites which the attentive analytic attitude of the therapist is requiring of him. He would seal this off within, intrapsychically, and simultaneously would seal it off without in the therapy interaction. Thus, the pressure that the therapist feels is precisely the same pressure for aberrant union, for obliteration of consciousness, which is the repressive force within the patient. The therapy space has become the interactional arena of the patient's otherwise hidden inner world or inner drama. The patient would obliterate the analytic consciousness and attitude of the therapist as he obliterates his potential analytic attitude toward his own unconscious processes. He wants the therapist to comply in forming such an obliterating aberrant union rather than to join in a mutual voyage through "the almost unendurable conflict" and "affliction of the soul" which a holding with these opposites and an exploration of the anxious feelings that span them would bring. He prefers instead the concrete—a cementing over—by means of simplifications, advice, intellectual formulae, statements of pseudo-understanding and pseudo-meaning. This would ensure, should the therapist comply, that the therapist and patient could then merge together at one level into a mutual sealing over and on a deeper level into an undifferentiated unconscious marriage in darkness.

Jung indentified this sort of union, which forgoes ego, as "an undifferentiated, unconscious state of primal being, . . . a condition [which] must be terminated, and as it is at the same time an object of regressive longing, it must be sacrificed in order that discriminated entities—i.e., conscious contents—may come into being" (1956, par. 650). "The instinctive desire . . . is given up in order that it may be regained in new form" (1956, par. 671). There is "the need for a discerning, evaluating, selecting, discriminating consciousness" (1956, par. 673). Jung also puts this in terms of the "incest prohibition" which "intervenes . . . for the purpose of canalizing the libido into new forms and effectively preventing it from regressing to actual incest" (1956, par. 332). This prohibition "acts as an obstacle and makes the creative fantasy inventive. . . . [It serves] to stimulate the creative imagination, which gradually opens up possible avenues for the self-realization of libido. In this way the libido becomes imperceptibly spiritualized" (1956, par. 332).

Another approach that Jung uses to deal with this clinical problem is to discuss boundaries. He emphasizes that the shadow, and the unconscious contents that follow it out of the realm of the archetypal, all share a common characteristic and that is that they "ride roughshod over all moral and any other human wishes and considerations" (1959, par. 370). The shadow of this patient would ride roughshod over the attempts of this therapist to "make creative fantasy inventive." This shadow, driven by anxiety, will have nothing of the human enterprise of soul-making. It will not be contained in "a protected *temenos*, a taboo area where he will be able to meet the unconscious" (1968, par. 63). Everywhere in his writings Jung insists that the establishment of a protected, boundaried space seems to be a crucial requirement for the productive use of *imaginatio*. And "*imaginatio* is the active evocation of . . . images, . . . an authentic feat of thought or ideation, which does not spin aimless and groundless fantasies 'into the blue' . . . but tries to grasp the inner facts and portray them in images true to their nature. This activity is an *opus*, a work" (1968, par. 219).

Imaginatio only occurs within a special and sacred space which contains the "*massa confusa*," the *materia* of the opus, and which is protected from the intrusion of the concrete, the literal, simplified, and intellectualized clichés and the many other forms of aberrant unions and manifold manifestations of incest. Each of these would obliterate the rich complexity and multilayered potentiality residing within the unconscious forces and bring tremendous relief from the tension of the opposites. This protected space needs to be watched over and carefully drawn with the therapist's attentive, devoted, and deliberate consciousness, which is aware of its rich gifts and its enormous fragility. By the direction and implications of his or her interventions, the therapist consciously is involved in "*the drawing of a spellbinding circle*" (emphasis added) (1968, par. 63). In this alone, *imaginatio* can safely occur.

The consciousness of the therapist in this interview is being challenged to perform once more for the patient this ancient act, which defines the essence of being human and guarantees that there will be a translation of the inchoate into the human, the symbolic. This is essentially the analytic attitude. It is an act that draws a line and holds that line—a line which says, "I will not respond in the kind you demand. There is another way for us to be together here, another way for us to communicate, another way for me to relate to the inchoate forces that upwell in you. I encourage, listen for, prepare the way for, and respond only to *imaginatio*, the great revealer, the spellbinder who draws you into the vast complexities of your own reality. I am *not* a counselor, advisor, teacher, judge, friend, or lover! I am different from all of these: rather I am the un-natural, the anti-natural. I am the drawer of the sacred spellbinding circle in which *imaginatio* will emerge and with that alone can you discover who you are. This is my task, this is the only union that I offer. This union I call a 'co-union,' a *coniunctio*, a union without unconscious fusions or aberrant unions."

The Therapist's Statement and the Patient's Perception and Reaction

Going back to the critical moment of erupting anxiety and interpersonal pressure in our example, we recall that the patient in this interview had ceased his explorations and image-making pre-maturely, had become anxious, and had wanted something concrete from the therapist. At such critical moments, a patient balks at the door leading into the symbolic therapy experience and would ask the therapist as well to close it and seal it with him. The therapist in this instance invited the patient to continue, offering the alchemical or analytical attitude, saying implicitly: "Let's continue with *imagin-atio*, this arduous and painful process of staying with the *massa confusa* and elevating the inchoate into the meaningful, of finding imagery and words, of creating a communicative marriage to this *prima materia* that is beginning to emerge here between us now in the form of anxiety."

Following Jung's interactional model, it is clear that some stimulus within this therapy has given rise to this anxiety-surrounded complex in the patient. We can ask ourselves what on earth the external stimulus has been; what action by the therapist has served as such a stimulus? The therapist has held to the the task of being there as an open, responsive, attentive consciousness who is oriented toward holding available the spellbinding circle for the patient's imaginary life. This is the only clear stimulus or action from the therapist. In inviting the patient to continue, the therapist takes a strong position. He contributes a vital ingredient to the interactional chemistry and becomes a stimulus for the patient's subsequent responses. His action and its underlying implications are taken into the psyche of the patient.

The patient's response will carry both the impression of this communication by the therapist as well as an unconscious perception of its full meaning. Jung himself saw the imagoes of the patient as a mixture of accurately perceived actualities of the patient's significant others, such as the parents, as well as the fantasied admix. When applied to therapy, we would say the patient experiences the therapist, or images the therapist, in an internal imago consisting of actual perception and an admixture of fantasy. Therefore, when the therapist completes a behavior or communication to a patient, he needs to scan consciously the subsequent imagery for each of these admixtures. Jung emphasized that the characteristics of every person portrayed in the images in a patient's associations, reminiscences, fantasies, and dreams may refer subjectively to the patient himself. But it is also clear that each of these may refer to the therapist as well. Let's look at Jung's words:

> I call every interpretation which equates the dream images with real objects an *interpretation on the objective level*. In contrast to this is the interpretation which refers every part of the dream and all the actors in it back to the dreamer himself. This I call *interpretation on the subjective level*. . . . It *detaches* the underlying memory-complexes from their external causes, regards them as *tendencies or components* [emphasis added] of the subject, and reunites them with that subject. . . . In this case, therefore, all contents of the dream are treated as symbols for subjective contents. (1966*b*, par. 129)

I would add to the "underlying complexes of memory," or of past conscious perception, the existence of *present unconscious perception* as well and the complexes that would affiliate with that perception. Jung seems to be saying that there are unconscious processes that attach, or associate, "tendencies or components" from one person to another, and he presents this attachment in narrative, fantasy, and dream. He is suggesting that consciously the therapist detaches these tendencies and components and reattaches them to the appropriate subject, i.e., the patient. I am making somewhat the same point in terms of process in that the tendencies and components may be detached and regarded as tendencies and components of the interactional field, which contains significant contributions by both therapist and patient. Consequently, the detached represented tendencies or components may refer equally to the therapist, to the patient and to others. The therapist's inputs or his or her "tendencies and components" are obviously of extreme importance, and he or she needs to consciously attach images of dream, fantasy, and narrative first to himself or herself to see if they reflect significant perceptions of their own behavior, which are in turn significantly shaping the interaction, before attaching them to the patient. Several Jungian analysts have recognized the importance of this principle of psychic functioning and use it in their practices (Goodheart, 1980, 1982, 1984; Groesbeck, 1983*a*, 1983*b*, 1984; Jaffe, 1982; Stevens, 1982*a*, 1982*b*).

With all this in mind, let's listen to the patient's response—this time in his own words—to the therapist's statement:

> "Everything in my life is going well. My business is successful, my relationship with my wife has a good sense about it. One boy is in college and doing well and another has a job and is working well there."

By using Jung's formula of "detaching tendencies and components," we come up with images of:

> business going well
> success
> good sense
> working well at a job.

Attach these tendencies and components to the therapist's specific preceding action, and we come up with a statement that the patient unconsciously perceived this action as *good, successful,* and working with *good sense.* The patient has perceived, taken in, and is reflecting back in this narrative and its images his full, unconscious experience of the therapist. It is not only a perception, however, but also an introjection—a taking in of a good object—and the experience has provided a microscopic increment of healing for the patient. It has provided the first foundation toward achieving some mastery over the seat of anxiety. At this point, the patient's comment is clearly an interactional product, for therapist and patient are in an intimate co-union. It is a transient moment; but it is there, and it is important. It is a small island of embryonic *coniunctio* for both of them amidst the sea of anxiety and unconscious pressures. It is important to note that the therapist had to do some internal work with himself to make this offering—the request that the patient say whatever came to his mind—to the patient. He had to get some distance from his own anxiety, to struggle to maintain his alchemical and analytic stance. The patient unconsciously appreciated this, and that appreciation is reflected in his response. This is not easy work for a therapist, and Winnicott beautifully captured its essence when he spoke of the "analytic strain."

The patient is experiencing this helpfulness from the therapist unconsciously. What is unconscious is severely split off from the conscious psyche. At this moment, then, the patient might well be consciously experiencing the therapist as extremely frustrating, even as a bad person, depriving and not giving him the explanations and directives he wants. In fact, we might say that it is precisely these critical moments that are ripe with the possibility of alchemical change because the split is being represented and the material opposed to the conscious state is being strongly carried in the images of the patient's associations. It is closer to the surface.

The therapist admitted later that he had wrestled aside the temptation to become a doctorly advisor and say: "Well you are near midlife, have had a distressing physical illness with even the confinement of hospitalization and all this has been a shock, maybe even forcing you to reevaluate your life. You've lost the old familiar footings, perhaps even experienced a brush with the terror of dying or of being helpless and not in control of things." Given the interactional situation of therapy and compared with the complexity of the actual reality existing between this patient and therapist, this fairly sophisticated explanatory statement is merely a cliché. It is this sort of statement that Jung seemed to despise when he speaks of attending to the patient's individuality, to the unique complexity and richness with images and symbols alone and of not reducing the patient to the simplistic formulations of directed thinking.

Indeed, to have used such a statement would have literally destroyed the uniqueness of the man, for it could be said of any middle-aged man who has been in a hospital and then developed neurotic symptoms. It is the sort of statement we make to one another as counselors, advisors, friends, and lovers. It carries no *imaginatio.* It abandons the analytic task. It is nearly meaningless. It could easily deliver a seductive, but false, implication that something significant had been said. It does nothing to make the unconscious conscious. What is it saying about the individual's unconscious life? Nothing. It totally abandons psyche, ignoring the tranformative interactional process going on between the therapist and the patient. It abandons the therapy as it abandons psyche. Nevertheless, such a statement might have brought conscious relief to the patient. Of course, that would have been short-lived and would have signaled to the patient's unconscious that his therapist was ready to abandon their respective souls to the isolating maneuvers of generalization and intellectualization whenever things got hot.

There are those who believe that the therapist needs to strengthen the ego of the patient first before the patient is ready to deal with the unconscious. Jungians and Freudians alike have distorted the meaning of strengthening the ego by implying it occurs by the therapist's being reassuring, supportive, lending the patient the therapist's ego or self, becoming an extraordinarily caring friend to the patient, or providing the patient with immediate and direct efforts to relieve psychic tension. This attitude leads some therapists into offering general intellectualizations, such as inferences about intrapsychic psychological, dynamic, and archetypal processes or into the giving of advice, the sharing of personal experiences, the sharing of objects, the touching of the patient physically, the hugging of the patient, and, in some instances, even into making love to the patient.

Proponents of such ego-strengthening measures maintain that they gather together the anxiety-ridden ego from its fragmentation out of an experience of object loss into a sense of being held or bonded together through the real experience of special connection, caring, or affection, free of any remoteness or glimmer of separateness, which the patient is not ready to tolerate and will experience as abandonment and isolation. Such advocates suggest that the therapist may from time to time need to offer the patient something other than the attentive, alchemical, analytic, symbol-honoring attitude, by abandoning the analytic attitude with its steadfast offering of *imaginatio* and by assuming the attitude of counselor, advisor, teacher, wise man or woman, judge, friend, or lover.

However, I contend that it is the therapist's *not* abandoning the analytic attitude which strengthens the patient's ego and experience of self, which aids the patient's capacity to hold himself or herself to a symbolic and reflecting attitude toward unconscious experiences in spite of what pressures there might be to do otherwise. Nonsymbolic attitudes and interventions by therapists usually ignore so much of what is happening in the dialectically interactional field that they essentially serve as solicitations by the therapist to deny or repress these realities from a relationship to consciousness. These denials and repressions weaken the patient's ego and split off significant dimensions of Self. Most compatible with Jung's view, I believe, is that as therapists we strengthen the patient's ego or increase the patient's capacity to maintain a field of consciousness toward the forces of the unconscious by ourselves holding to the symbolic-analytic attitude, which alone is capable of making the unconscious conscious, of transmuting the products of the primitive and undifferentiated unconscious affects and images of the total Self into consciousness. And each increment of this that is achieved lends and consolidates strength to the ego of the patient. By maintaining this symbolic attitude and communicating in that mode regardless of the interactional pressures to do otherwise, we provide a model of sound ego-functioning and the strength for individuation, which the patient will introject or feel unconsciously. We signal to the patient that we know he or she has a Self hidden within, which will and can join us in this enterprise.

The Triggering of the Patient's Neurosis

In the clinical sequence described above, the patient followed the therapist's statement with a commentary of unconscious recognition of the value and good sense of the therapist's attending to the analytic attitude and offering it to the patient. Immediately following this request that he continue to say whatever came to his mind, the patient's anxiety mounted, and he suddenly asked permission to smoke. In a microcosm, we can see his problem: He cannot tolerate being offered—and involved in—a nondisturbed relationship, an embryonic developing *coniunctio*, where each is committed to a mutual symbolic search and exploration. Such an approaching involvement, and his experience of it, awakens in him unsettling anxieties.

A core issue in neurosis is the inability to tolerate a wholesome relationship without the emergence of powerful, primitive, and even archetypal terrors and the applying of pressure on others for relief from such terrors, usually by asking them to join in an aberrant union that will destroy the first strands of a developing *coniunctio*. Proponents of ego-strengthening assume that neurotically suffering individuals suffer because they have never had the opportunity for a wholesome relationship and that the cure of the neurosis is that the therapist offers healing solely by making such a relationship available. It is more complicated than this, however, for neurotically suffering individuals are not able to tolerate and allow to go undisturbed the opportunities for wholesome relationships which are available to them within their environment. Neurotics suffer from never having had an opportunity for such a relationship *and* from unconscious forces that repetitively and powerfully destroy or avoid any potentially wholesome relationship they may encounter or engage. Therefore, the therapist's task is threefold: (a) to make such a relationship again available to the patient; (b) to be able to withstand the anxieties and associated solicitations, invitations, and pressures from the patient which will begin to emerge as he tries to persuade the therapist in various ways to alter and skew the potentiality of the analytic co-union into an aberrant union; and (c) to interpret to the patient an empathic comprehension of the patient's anxieties and dread of the co-union and his or her destructive avoidant and unwholesome efforts toward it.

The patient's severe anxieties and his request to smoke seem in this light to be a response to the therapist's offering the patient a wholesome *coniunctio* and individuation-bound relationship. His anxiety does not arise out of a state of deprivation and loss of object-relatedness.

Creating an Interpretation:
The Marriage of *Imaginatio* and Interaction

The therapist is in a tough place. He has very little information to go on. He sees that his patient is in severe distress and is seeking some direct, nonsymbolic relief outside of the spellbinding circle. He wishes desperately for a nonanalytic, nonsymbolic experience. This is a classically difficult therapy situation that epitomizes one of the major dilemmas in the practice of alchemical therapy: how to give the patient the experience of the analytic attitude with its attendant meaning and the full embracing of the patient's inner split through imagery from the unconscious when there is very little imagery or symbol present and there is considerable pressure from the patient for another type of attitude and communication from the therapist. Because this particular case is so stark, it affords us a marvelous opportunity to study the framework of how we might bring meaning to the patient and bind together the patient's inner split while following Jung's insistence that therapy is a chemical combination of two psychic systems and requires the establishment of the spellbinding circle.

At this point had I been the therapist I might have chosen to formulate an intervention by throwing together in the following skeletal way all that has occurred:

1. I behaved in such and such a way.

2. This influenced you, you perceived it and took it in, or introjected it.

3. You have come up in *imaginatio* with images, or tendencies and components, which are attachable to the persons portrayed, to yourself, and, most importantly, to me—as a response to my behavior.

4. You are becoming aware of symptoms or psychic disturbance around this experience of my behavior, as a response to it. You have valid unconscious perceptions of it and its meanings as well as disturbed and creative fantasy constellations. We don't know about the latter as yet though.

After analyzing the situation this far, I would then make a statement such as the following to the patient.

"You know, we have been together a few minutes and something about me and our meeting here is making you anxious. Out of your anxiety, you found it hard to continue and wanted some suggestions or directives from me. This might have relieved your uncertainty, but I encouraged you to go on saying whatever came to your mind. You then presented images of working well, of successes, and of good sense, which might well have been a response to my encouragement to you to continue. Part of you appreciated it, but part of you always becomes anxious in spite of things going well, so here, too, you became puzzled when you realized your anxiety erupted right after that appreciation, making you feel uncomfortable; it was even painful to you, and you wanted some relief: that's when you thought of smoking. So you asked me for permission to smoke, much as you asked me to answer your questions for directions or advice. Getting such questions answered relieved your anxieties for awhile, as smoking does. In a way, you'd like me to answer your questions, but on another level you sort of appreciated the fact that I did not answer you directly but encouraged you to continue. On this basis, it seems best that you continue to say whatever comes to mind—rather than our doing things directly to immediately relieve your anxiety—and let's see what comes up. Then we'll begin to understand the nature and source of these anxious feelings that are so interfering with your life."

I am trying to state realistically in my interpretation how the therapist and patient both mutually and reciprocally contributed to the process as well as how the patient perceived unconsciously their interaction by using his own imagery and language. I have sought to show how the patient's symptoms were triggered by the interaction and were linked to the therapist's specific behavior.

The therapist starts, then, with a careful and detailed circumambulating around the interactional process—this mutual product and reality which both therapist and patient share and have contributed to in that moment. Once he feels that he has been fair to this, he cautiously begins to make inferences about the patient's intrapsychic life and where that might be revealed in his imagery, narratives, dreams, and fantasies. He tries not to make inferences or statements about the patient's intrapsychic life without such material, since such inferences can serve easily as abandoning intellectualizations to the yet-unknown and split-off parts of the patient's psyche. If the patient has not given the therapist this information, he is not ready to do so. Whatever threat the therapist is or represents needs to be first brought into language and consciousness, and the patient will pace this unconsciously as the therapist proves reliable in being able to wait and then lift it into consciousness for him.

The Triggering of the Therapist's Neurosis

Unfortunately, this therapist could not hold to the spellbinding circle when he was met with the pressure of the patient's severe anxiety and the direct request to allow smoking. In a state of internal distress, or "psychic infection," he likewise became severely anxious, needed relief himself, and took out an ashtray and handed it to the patient! The therapist could not contain the initial *nigredo,* the first meeting of the opposites of conscious and unconscious, and bring the sacred spellbinding circle of attentive inquiry toward *imaginatio* to the patient's emerging unconscious, which in this instance was in the form of immediate demands and pressuring anxiety. The therapist joined with the patient in a moment of "aberrant natural union of opposites," of Jung's warned-against concrete, nonsymbolic fusion and an abandonment of the alchemical process and its initial steps toward a co-union or *coniunctio* and individuation. This is what Jung meant by the phrase "falling victim to the shadow." Here, in this moment, the therapist failed those demands of higher consciousness required of the analyst-alchemist. He was not able to keep the "discerning, evaluating, selecting, discriminating consciousness" necessary to carry out the opus. Let's see again how the patient responds:

> "Business is going pretty well, but I don't trust my partners. They don't seem to have the ability to make solid decisions; they often seem anxious, and at critical times too. I'm not too sure of them. I don't like being physically ill. I don't quite know what is going on. The doctors have done all they could. They want to give me Valium, but I really don't want to go that route. But maybe there is a medicine that would help me. Look here, I really have to get this under control fast, it is interfering with my business. In fact, I want to get this cleared up by next week. What do you think is going on, and can you help me now? Would you suggest something?"

Let's follow Jung's suggestion of "detach[ing] the underlying memory-complexes from their external causes, regard[ing] them as tendencies or components of the subject, and reunit[ing] them with that subject" (1966b, par. 129). However, in this instance it is quite clear that the most critical subject in this interaction is the person of the therapist during his last intervention, and the memory is the current unconscious perception, the instantaneous memory, of this interaction and behavior. In detaching, then, the tendencies or components attributed to the partners, we get:

partners
lack of ability to make solid decisions
often being anxious, especially at critical times.

In detaching the tendencies or components ascribed to the patient himself, we find he is:

not knowing what is going on.

In detaching the tendencies or components of the doctors, as well as the image of "doctors," we find:

doctors
want to give Valium, a chemical antianxiety agent.

Following Jung's subjective level of interpretation, but choosing the therapist as the subject (since it is his behavior that the patient has just introjected and to which the patient is responding), we hear a remarkably cogent commentary on the underlying meaning and significance of the action of the therapist. Paraphrased, the patient is *unconsciously* saying to the therapist:

> You are not to be trusted as a partner, for you lack the ability to remain solidly behind your decision to encourage me to say whatever comes to my mind or to be a therapist because you become anxious at critical times and don't seem to know what is going on. In fact, you end up wanting to soothe my anxieties, and that means yours as well, by handing me an ashtray and encouraging me to take chemical antianxiety agents into my mouth, bloodstream, and brain. You are one of those kinds of doctors.

Though *consciously* relieved and maybe even appreciative of this act of apparent benevolence and "natural union" by the therapist, the patient *unconsciously* is quite upset about this failing on his therapist's part. *His overt symptom, anxiety, remains the same, but the dynamics underlying it have radically changed!*

We really haven't discovered what specifics from his inner world have awakened his anxiety as he entered into this wholesome relationship that the therapist initially offered. But now he is in the care of a therapist whom he unconsciously distrusts *for valid reasons and not for projected, imagined, or transference reasons only!* The patient's anxiety is now in good part *appropriate* and no longer symptomatic. Our whole approach to understanding the patient's anxiety must shift 180 degrees at this moment, for it was his anxiety that was predominant; now it is the therapist's. The therapist's anxiety has compelled him to undermine and abandon his task and mandate as an alchemical analyst. The therapist's act was a neurotic act, by all definitions of the term, and Jung's is as good as any:

> ... we can no longer explain neurosis by the development of certain fantasy systems. The really explanatory approach now is a prospective one.... We ask rather: What is the task which the patient does not want to fulfil? What difficulty is he trying to avoid? (1961, par. 409)

"The patient" is now, of course, the therapist, who is not able to fulfill the task of therapy, of holding to the spellbinding circle, of preparing the arena for *imaginatio*. And yet, this is the very task he has asked the patient to hold to.

Now the patient's unconscious has not only perceived the true nature of this act by the therapist and communicated its perception, but has introjected as well the entire thrust and implication of the act, which is to sanction and encourage the patient to handle anxiety by finding immediate relief, even chemical relief. Another part of the patient's unconscious, a compensating and rectifying part, recognizes that this is inimical to his treatment and that the therapist had better get this under some sort of management, or the analytical task and the patient's path toward individuation will founder. This part of the patient's unconscious then offers to the therapist corrective and compensatory statements in the associations in order to guide the therapist to a more helpful attitude.

We have learned from Jung that the unconscious brings forth compensatory efforts toward certain one-sidedness or complex-possessedness present in the individual's ego-functioning. When the patient introjects such a psychic constellation from the therapist, his own unconscious likewise will bring forth compensatory efforts toward that psychic constellation. These efforts will appear in the patient's associations and can be viewed as *highly cogent unconscious efforts to conduct a therapy on the therapist*.

Consequently, we can detach further "therapeutic" messages directed toward the therapist:

> I don't want to go that route.
> Get this under control fast, it is interfering with my business.
> I want this cleared up.

Jung intuitively knew this:

It is an open secret that all through the analysis . . . patients are looking beyond it into the soul of the analyst, in order to find there the confirmation of the healing formulae—or its opposite. It is quite impossible, even by the subtlest analysis, to prevent the patient from taking over instinctively the way in which the analyst deals with the problems of life. (1961, par. 447)

The Myth of the Innocent Observer-Interpreter

The approach to therapy I am presenting here flows inevitably, in my opinion, from much of Jung's basic postulates and discoveries. To follow through into actual practice using these viewpoints makes great demands on the therapist, demands which could not even be conceived, let alone mastered, by Freud or Jung. It seems to me that only now after a century of sober monitoring of the analytic process, of scrutinizing successes, failures, and stalemates, and of the steady enrichment of the analytic consciousness are we able to begin applying the full consequences and implications of Jung's theoretical view of the two psychic systems in reciprocal interaction into the actual practice of Jungian analysis. Foremost, this requires a rigorous discipline of a well-trained consciousness and a readiness of the therapist to live with the experience of the patient's continuously outlining starkly and irrefutably within free association, active imagination, and disturbed behavior the most conflict laden and personally painful weaknesses of the therapist.

For some time, Jungians shared with other psychoanalytic approaches a fundamental assumption in their practices and in their case presentations of the myth of the innocent observer-interpreter (see Langs 1982; Racker 1972; and Szasz 1963). The myth states that the therapist is thought to be basically "innocent" of much that happens within the interactional space of therapy as well as within the intrapsychic spaces of the patient. What occurs there is seen as occurring autonomously against the background provided by a stable and facilitating therapist who may falter now and then. Generally, then, interpretations or comments to the patient take the form of pointing out patterns of behavior or "complex" or "unconscious" constellations that the patient is experiencing or struggling with. "*You* are experiencing such and such" or "*your* unconscious is now dealing with or manifesting such and such" are the sorts of statements that do not articulate the full reality of an interactional field. They subtly presuppose the events within the patient as being at most tangentially linked to the therapist's behavior. They are not truly interactional. A better articulation of the interactional process would be: "I have done such and such. You perceived and experienced me as illuminated in your imagery and behavior in this specific and complex way, and now, as a result, you are experiencing or dealing with such and such, or else you wish to or you are behaving in such and such a way."

Jung, more than any other psychoanalytic and psychological contributor of his generation, was able to work himself partially free from that myth and envision the full interactional nature of the therapy process as being "of such intensity that we could almost speak of a 'combination.' When two chemical substances combine, both are altered" (1966a, par. 358). However, Jung did not speak consistently from this "combination" viewpoint when he gave specific examples from his practice, nor have many of his followers. Most commonly a brief acknowledgment is given to the interactional *mixtum compositum* of therapist and patient, or to the view that the therapist and patient are both present in the alchemical container and part of the process, and then the majority of focus goes on to what is happening *inside* the patient, intrapsychically, in terms of the unfolding images, dreams, and affects emanating from the patient's unconscious. Quite often, then, the interactional realities between therapist and patient are not explored at all or are assumed to be of negligible importance or are simply assumed to provide a good container for the patient's inner process. There is a failure to bring an equally intense focus and conscious relationship to the ongoing and multilayered complex realities of the "two psychic systems in interaction." Too easily this arduous task is bypassed and neglected in favor of a one-sided approach through the intrapsychic perspective alone. This fails to adequately deal with those unconscious forces within the patient and the therapist which pressure for and succeed in establishing a nonanalytic, actually incestuous and aberrant union in reality within the therapy relationship. This aberrant union then concretizes in mutual collaboration between therapist and patient significant unconscious material in such a way that it will not be lifted into image and consciousness unless careful exploration and understanding of the interactional realities are achieved. In some cases, then, the purely symbolic approach to therapy is unconsciously grounded on an aberrant union and receives its driving energy not from a creative relationship to the unconscious but from an inflated and intoxicating acting-out of the patient's fusion experience through the release of striking and dramatic unfoldings of released images, fantasy, and dream. They gain their impelling force through the relief achieved from not having to deal with the interactional *nigredo* phase of the individuation process.

Also, and from a somewhat different perspective, a recent writer pointed out how the therapist must be on guard that he not be the one who "establishes a contract with . . . patients in which the patients bring their intense experiences of living and [the therapist] translates these into fantasies for them" (Khan 1978, p. 260). He continues: "Such interpretation of fantasies creates a pseudopsychic reality, to which the patient gets addicted. This leads to those interminable deep analyses which we often hear about these days" (Khan 1978, p. 263).

In another paper, I summarized Jung's explorations of the rudimentary origins of the imaginary-symbolic life in the developmental stages of the infant: "Symbolizing always presupposes a certain acceptance of the inability to re-obtain in reality the original 'incestuous' state for which the individual once regressively clamored" (Goodheart 1981, pp. 14–15). To accept this inability, the patient must be frustrated, on the one hand, from obtaining in actuality the incestuous and natural aberrant union for which part of his or her unconscious life clamors; on the other hand, the patient must receive the human and compassionate meeting with the therapist who brings understanding, comprehension of the widely disparate and opposing needs of the patient, and the firm stance toward the awakening and emergence of *imaginatio*. This step is an enormous, fundamental one, which Jung portrays as ". . . the attempt to free the ego-consciousness from the deadly grip of the unconscious" (1956, par. 539) or as the movement away "from getting stuck in the material corporeality of the mother" (1956, par. 510).

In our clinical vignette, this would be the analyst's holding off from giving the patient the ashtray and from even agreeing or not agreeing that it is all right for the patient to smoke. The issue is not one of agreeing or forbidding: The issue is the elevation of the urge and request to smoke into symbolic comprehension. The therapist is struggling to free the patient from this particular deadly grip of the unconscious and the material corporeality of the mother. The therapist's task is to gain access to their *"symbolic equivalent"* (emphasis added) (1956, par. 522) and present it to the patient.

In therapy this is always a moment of extreme tension, for we are dealing with a truly "deadly grip." The therapist holds the request in abeyance, tolerates the tension which that brings, and then must provide as well an interpretation that will serve as a symbolic equivalent and replacement for the sacrifice and loss the patient is suffering from giving up this particular longed for aberrant union and the relief it would immediately bring. This replacement is a magnificent composite gift of several embodied achievements of the therapist. There is the therapist's capacity to forgo his or her need for the more natural and anxiety-relieving aberrant union and clinging to the "material corporeality of the mother." There is the therapist's being able to offer from a more individuated state than the patient—in the midst of the regressive clamoring demand and infecting anxiety—an interpretation. This is a unique and creative product of the therapist's understanding, of empathic response and symbolic comprehension, of his or her own *imaginatio* and soul. This gift carries the complexity of the patients' experiences back to them in their own images and symbols of meaning, creatively ordered in such a way as to illuminate for them their reality and the reality which they share with their therapist and the therapist's empathic, actual, and transferentially distorted reality. It humanizes the former undifferentiated forces that made up these realities. With this effort the patient is held in a web of meaning, empathy, and mutual symbolic understanding. This is a moment of co-union, embryonic *coniunctio*, for the patient and therapist. It is the crux of a nonaberrant union, of an unnatural union—a union *contra naturam*. The giving of the ashtray was a moment of aberrant and natural union, a moment of physical incest, a moment of both being stuck in the deadly grip of the material corporeality of the mother, which temporarily destroys the spellbinding circle.

The Interactional Birth of the Concepts of "Transference" and of "Autonomous Psyche"

The early founders of the psychoanalytic situation were entering for the first time into the most intimate relationship with another person ever established by mankind. The demands on the psyches of these men and women were enormous, for they had no precedents to guide them and no previous framework of understanding with which to find a footing. They cast themselves adrift into the chaotic upwellings of their own and their patients' inner worlds which emerged within this unique, private, intimate, and intense contact with patients. They faced and had to find some sort of reconciliation with raw psychic forces which previously had been faced square on only by those on private voyages of malignant or creative insanity. We know well of the suicides and violent and destructive schisms that developed among these pioneers.

For example, we well know and understand now the emotional chaos which Joseph Breuer, the first pioneer, experienced. He attended to Anna O, and she guided him into the value of the "talking cure." Yet Breuer's unconscious erotic involvement with her led her into becoming for him an unconscious replacement for his mother, who had died when he was quite young. And he became a replacement for her recently lost father, an erotic laden replacement. They both discovered a rudimentary path to *imaginatio*. But they foundered severely by confusing and mixing physical attending and symbolic interpreting and transforming. The entire experience collapsed, therefore, into an erotic intoxication of being bound mutually in a love relationship disguised as therapy but which was in reality an aberrant union within the deadly grip of the unconscious. As Breuer began to be aware of only a small fraction of what was really going on, he had to flee. Anna O's entire life was skewed by this experience. She required a psychiatric hospitalization and relief from morphine addiction to which Breuer had inadvertently introduced her, and she spent the rest of her life unmarried and dedicated to the service of exploited and abused women.

Sigmund Freud, pupil and admirer of Breuer, was horrified at the outcome of this first use of the "talking cure." Yet he also had seen its healing potential. He approached it extremely cautiously thereafter, always fully aware of what had happened to Breuer. He waited for several years before trying it himself. When he finally did begin his work with patients in this way, he too began to sense the cauldron of formerly repressed primitive emotions and images emerging. In the midst of the eroticized gestures toward him, Freud suddenly found a solution, a footing, a way to get some distance and separation (which Breuer did not have) from these experiences. In the midst of the emerging emotions and images, he suddenly came upon the notion that these erotic feelings directed toward him were "false connections" (Breuer and Freud 1895; see also Langs 1982). They had no valid connection to him and really belonged or connected somewhere else, and that, he suddenly realized, must be to the primary figures in the patient's early life: Freud gleaned the notion that there was somehow an unresolved family romance being reenacted inappropriately upon him. This was a brilliant intuition, and out of it grew his groundbreaking concept of the "transference." But, at the very moment it was conceived, the concept was also serving as a relieving, defensive intellectualization that isolated Freud himself from the full reality of his actual erotic involvements and contributions to the interactional processes occurring between him and his patients! For Freud was in reality a charming, urbane, and strongly conflicted man sexually (Roazen 1974). He probably was seductive with his patients, perhaps unconsciously, far more than he realized and derived some erotic gratification and release through his work with them. Therefore, his patients' sexual feelings toward him were in part appropriate responses to the reality he unconsciously presented to them. Freud's concept of transference was, then, partly a defensive denial and partly a repressive force against the full realization of his full interaction with his patients.

Jung entered this new world of the analytic situation beset with all of his unresolved inner conflicts. He was much younger and less experienced than Freud and had not had the sobering firsthand experience of a Breuer to serve as a warning guide. He was strongly ingrained with a Swiss puritanism which had not allowed him to integrate considerable unconscious erotic conflicts and he was filled with determination to prove the existence of a spiritual dimension of the psyche. It seems clear that he was thrown into the chaotic upwellings of his own conflicted inner world as well as that of his patients. Like Freud, Jung needed to gain some footing and distance for himself, and Jung achieved this by coming up with the brilliant formulation of the "autonomous psyche." This became the foundation later on for his mature concepts of the "reality of the psyche" and the "collective unconscious." This formulation provided him from the beginning with the firm footing and distance that he needed, much as the concept of transference served Freud. And, too, as with Freud, Jung's concept was born partly as a defensive, isolating, and intellectualized construct to help him deny and repress the full realization of his own unconscious contributions and participation in his patients' instinctual and other complex-ridden experiences and their mutual interactional realities. Where Freud could ground the roots of the unfolding experience of the patient elsewhere than in the interaction, that is in a "family romance," so Jung was able to ground these roots in a "mythological romance," so to speak. In this way both men removed themselves to a major degree from recognizing themselves as fully responsible and as ongoing contributors to the interactional fields and the intrapsychic fields of their patients. To postulate transference or the autonomous psyche in isolation as a prime mover in the therapy situation is to invoke the myth of the innocent observer-interpreter. Neither Freud nor Jung believed totally in this myth. Jung in fact challenged it more consistently than did Freud, and it was one of the issues he emphasized in his split with Freud. Yet, like Freud, he implicitly assumed this myth when he wrote about his patients and when he described how he thought about his patients. This is not surprising, for these early founders had to find some stable fulcrum on which they could rely and from which they could make observations and build comments to make to their patients. They needed that myth desperately in their clinical work, and because of the stability and distance which that myth provided, the analytic situation could come into being and the needed distance between patient and therapist which Breuer had lost could be held.

One can see this most clearly in Jung's first paper, his dissertation, "On the Psychology and Pathology of So-called Occult Phenomena" (1970c, pars. 1–165). Here Jung clearly constructed the concept of the "autonomous psyche" at precisely the points where he needed to deny that an erotically infused relationship did exist between himself and the subject or "patient" of that particular study, who was actually his cousin, Helene Preiswerk. With the concept of the autonomous psyche introduced, he could maintain that his actual presence and actions had little or no influence and made no contribution toward the upwelling of rich erotic and incestuous fantasies and subpersonalities which she was producing and that there was not a significant cause and effect relationship between himself and her emotional and psychic imaginary life (Goodheart 1984).

Freud, Jung, and the next generation of their followers needed the myth of the innocent observer-interpreter as a foundation upon which to begin an investigation of the nature and treatability of the wounded human psyche. Thanks to their work and the profound enrichment of consciousness, of *analytic* consciousness, which we have inherited from them, we no longer need this myth.

It has been exactly one hundred years since Breuer first saw Anna O., and over 80 years since Jung first saw Helene Preiswerk. Because of their pioneering efforts and the foundations they laid, we have been able to heighten and stretch our consciousness of ourselves as analysts and therapists to the point where we are beginning to be able to tolerate the irrefutable fact that *patients are unconsciously monitoring the total underlay and implications of the therapist's behaviors and communications.* We are learning that therapists' behavior and communication are infused with unconscious instinctual, archetypal, and defensive needs that are obstructive to the analytic process and the full individuation of the patient. We are learning that patients not only unconsciously perceive and portray these needs in their associations as tendencies and components attributed to various figures of reminiscences, fantasies, and dreams, but unconsciously make efforts to communicate correcting and compensating images and behaviors to their therapists in an attempt to heal them.

Jung discussed unconscious perception in some detail in his earliest work and saw it as part of the most fundamental organizing texture of the unconscious psyche, a dimension that lay solidly below all splits and dissociations (1970c, par. 130). He laid the theoretical foundations in that first article for a further articulation of this process when the individual is engaged in intense interactions. But he dropped it, just as Freud dropped it. To pursue it would have led to an undermining and collapse of the myth of the innocent observer-interpreter, which simply would have been impossible at that early stage of laying the foundations for the analytic enterprise. Since analysis had not yet been created, how could we expect these early founders to enter into a subtle process of analysis of themselves through their patients' unconscious productions and efforts? On what firm ground could they have then stood in order to begin to investigate psyche? The Archemedian point *was* that the therapist was healthier than the patient generally, and standing on that ground, trusting in that, the therapist had the right to make inferences about what was happening inside the patient and could make interpretations. *Now,* the Archemedian point states that part of the patient's unconscious is healthier than the therapist or at least makes healthy commentaries on the more unwholesome or disturbed efforts of the therapist. It is to this that the therapists of today can attune themselves and in this that they can place their final trust:

> Between doctor and patient, therefore, there are imponderable factors which bring about a mutual transformation. In the process, the stronger and more stable personality will decide the final issue. . . . The doctor is as much "in the analysis" as the patient. He is equally a part of the psychic process of treatment and therefore equally exposed to the transforming influences. . . . The doctor is therefore faced with the same task which he wants his patient to face. (1966a, pars. 164, 166, 167)

I would like to conclude by presenting what I feel would be the most helpful and therapeutic sort of "symbolic equivalent" or interpretation to our patient at this point. It emerges from the full embracing of the reciprocal-interactional paradigm which is implicit in Jung's thought but which he could not embody in his practical clinical work with patients in the complete manner accessible to us today:

> "You know, I'd been encouraging you to just go ahead and say whatever came to your mind, for in that way we could best proceed and discover and learn something about these things you are suffering from. And when I did that—so encouraged you—you followed by speaking of things being quite stable and solid generally, and this may have given an image of how you experienced my inviting you to continue—as being stabilizing and solid. But then you became anxious and asked if you could smoke. And instead of my going further in encouraging you to speak more about what came to mind about the anxiety you were feeling and about the need for a cigarette, I *gave* you, *handed* you directly, an ashtray and in that way encouraged you to relieve your anxiety by smoking.
>
> Now this did bring relief to you, but then you went on to speak about not trusting your partners. We certainly are partners here, and you are indicating that you experienced my handing you that ashtray as something to be distrusted in me, for you then followed with images of partners being anxious and unreliable at critical times. That moment of your asking for the cigarette was a critical time between us, and you are saying that you experienced me as being anxious and unreliable in doing that. You went on with the images of 'not knowing what to do' and of doctors who would treat anxiety with chemical agents, and this could equally reflect that you indirectly began to feel that I didn't know what I was doing when I handed you that ashtray and that like those doctors you disapprove of I would solve this difficulty with anxiety, this anxiousness in you and in me, by encouraging you to take a cigarette, a chemical agent, to solve this problem temporarily. You are really saying on this dimension that you didn't like this behavior of mine, that it is interfering with our business here, you want me to cease it, and you at this level do not want to smoke either as a temporary solution to your anxiety and my anxiety."

This has been a specific application of how I understand and apply in my practice of Jungian analysis Jung's famous declaration on the dialectic process of analysis:

> The demand that the analyst must be analysed culminates in the idea of a dialectical procedure, where the therapist enters into relationship with another psychic system both as questioner and answerer. No longer is he the superior wise man, judge, and counsellor; he is a fellow participant who finds himself involved in the dialectical process just as deeply as the so-called patient. (1966a, par. 8)

References

Breuer, Jr., and Freud, S. 1895. *Studies on hysteria.* In *Standard edition*, vol. 2, pp. 1–305. London: Hogarth Press.

Goodheart, W. 1980. Theory of analytic interaction. *The San Francisco Jung Institute Library Journal* 1:2–39.

_____. 1981. Between reality and fantasy. *The San Francisco Jung Institute Library Journal* 2:1–24.

_____. 1982. Review of *The supervisory experience,* by Robert Langs. *Quadrant* 15:73–75.

_____. 1984. Jung's first "patient"—On the seminal emergence of Jung's thought. *Journal of Analytical Psychology* 29:1.

Groesbeck, C. J. 1983a. Freud and Jung—Similarities and differences. Presented at Freud-Jung Symposium, Langley Porter Psychiatric Institute, University of California Medical Center, San Francsico. Proceedings to be published.

_____. 1983b. Review of *A secret symmetry: Sabina Spielrein between Jung and Freud,* by A. Carotenuto. *Psychological Perspectives* 14/1:89–99.

_____. 1984. Carl Jung. In *Comprehensive textbook of psychiatry,* 4th ed., H. I. Kaplan and B. J. Sadock, eds., chap. 9.3. Baltimore: Williams & Wilkins.

Jaffe, L. 1982. From the ridiculous to the sublime: A desultory introduction to the psychology of Robert Langs. (Address to the Psychotherapy Institute, Berkeley, Calif.) *Psychotherapy Institute Journal* 1/1:24–31.

Jung, C. G. 1956. *Symbols of transformation.* In *Collected works*, vol. 5. Princeton: Princeton University Press.

_____. 1959. *Aion: Researches into the phenomenology of the self.* In *Collected works*, vol. 9, ii. Princeton: Princeton University Press.

_____. 1961. *Freud and psychoanalysis.* In *Collected works*, vol. 4. Princeton: Princeton University Press.

_____. 1966a. *The practice of psychotherapy.* In *Collected works*, vol. 16. Princeton: Princeton University Press.

_____. 1966b. *Two essays on analytical psychology.* In *Collected works*, vol. 7. Princeton: Princeton University Press.

_____. 1968. *Psychology and alchemy.* In *Collected works*, vol. 12. Princeton: Princeton University Press.

_____. 1970a. *Civilization in transition.* In *Collected works*, vol. 10. Princeton: Princeton University Press.

_____. 1970b. *Mysterium coniunctionis.* In *Collected works*, vol. 14. Princeton: Princeton University Press.

_____. 1970c. *Psychiatric studies.* In *Collected works*, vol.1. Princeton: Princeton University Press.

Khan, M. Masud R. 1978. Secret as potential space. In *Between reality and fantasy,* S. A. Grolnick & L. Barkin, eds., pp. 257–69. New York: Jason Aronson.

Langs, R. 1982. *The psychotherapeutic conspiracy.* New York: Jason Aronson.

Racker, H. 1972. The meanings and use of countertransference. *Psychiatric Quarterly* 41:487–506.

Roazen, P. 1974. *Freud and his followers.* New York: New American Library.

Stevens, B. 1982*a.* A critical assessment of the work of Robert Langs. *The San Francisco Jung Institute Library Journal* 3:1–36.

————. 1982*b.* An exchange of letters with R. Langs. *The San Francisco Jung Institute Library Journal* 3:55–60.

Szasz, T. 1963. The concept of transference. *International Journal of Psychoanalysis* 44:432–43.

Reflections on the Transference/ Countertransference Process with Borderline Patients

Harriet Gordon Machtiger

And the end of all our exploring
Will be to arrive where we started
And know the place for the first time.
T. S. Eliot, "Little Gidding"

The practice of analytical psychology is still in its formative stages. Jung himself espoused an empirical openness to new ideas, accepted and encouraged change, and stressed the importance of one's own experience in arriving at a particular theoretical stance. As Jungians, we need to constantly evaluate and reevaluate our mode of therapeutic interaction and be willing to absorb and implement theoretical changes.

My thoughts for this paper arose out of clinical work with a number of patients who showed many features of the borderline disorder. Jungian analysis holds a great attraction for individuals in

Harriet Gordon Machtiger, Ph.D., is a Jungian analyst practicing in Pittsburgh, Pennsylvania. A diplomate of the University of London Child Development Center, she received her Ph.D. in psychology from the University of London. An associate trainee in child psychotherapy at the Tavistock Clinic who completed Jungian training at the British Association of Psychotherapists, she is a member of the New York Association of Analytical Psychologists and of the Inter-Regional Society of Jungian Analysts. She is the author of "Countertransference/Transference" in *Jungian Analysis* (M. Stein, ed., 1982).

this particular plight, as they see in Jung a legitimization of their personal psychology. The patients who gave rise to the thoughts expressed in this paper contributed greatly to my growth as a person and as an analyst.

The creative encounter of the analytic process, by its interaction with another human being, can facilitate the corrective emotional experience that is a prerequisite for the growth and development necessary for the movement from borderline to higher level functioning. In the borderline there was a primary environmental failure because of chronic and repetitive parental failures to meet the particular constellation of maturational needs presented by the patient in infancy and early childhood. These early pathological relationships are likely to be superimposed, sooner or later, on all subsequent emotionally significant relationships. This leads to further failure and intrapsychic and interpersonal warping. Persons coming to treatment bring their different ways of experiencing themselves and others, or their subjective phenomenological frames of reference, to the analytic situation. This subjective experience is reenacted in the relational process of the transference/countertransference. Borderline patients have already had a maturational failure in childhood. Since they have such difficulty with interpersonal relatedness, they run a distinct danger of experiencing a second maturational failure in therapy, unless the analyst is able to respond in a developmentally appropriate way.

The term *borderline* is not a clear diagnostic condition or entity. There is no such thing as a unitary borderline condition. It is a descriptive title for a rather broad category of individuals with arrested psychological development. The syndrome has been perceived as a deficiency illness (Balint 1968; Harding 1965). According to Kohut (1971), the borderline patient has specific disturbances in the realm of the self. Objects are not experienced as being separate and independent from the self. The fixation points are located at a rather early point in psychic development. There is a defect in ego functioning. Grinker and Dry (1968) cite the clinical manifestations and characteristics of the patients and note the fears of aggression in themselves and others, the fear of loving and of being close, of tenuous interpersonal relationships, and of deficient reality orientation. There is a greater than usual use of denial and projection, a proneness to acting out, becoming promiscuous, and using drugs to excess. In the view of Knight (1954), the borderline case is one in which the normal ego functions and defenses against primitive unconscious impulses are severely weakened.

Jung (1946) approaches the borderline state from the perspective of Janet's notion of an *abaissement du niveau mental.* There is a disintegration and lowering of the threshold of consciousness and the intrusion of archaic contents that are not sufficiently inhibited. When consciousness disintegrates, the complexes are simultaneously freed from restraint and break through into ego consciousness. The *abaissement* denotes the loss of supremacy of the ego, after a struggle with unconscious contents and forces. Jung's formulation is useful in that it cuts across the problems of nosological classification. The *abaissement* is found in the neuroses as well as in the psychoses. It is a difference in degree, a qualitative and quantitative state, rather than the crossing of a hypothetical line. It is a continuum in which in the neuroses, the unity of the personality is at least potentially preserved.

The patient's problem arises from the lack of integration and adaptation to reality. There is an inability to tolerate anxiety, impulses, fears, and guilt feelings. The central conflict in distinguishing between the self and the outside world is fraught with ambivalence and permeated by the fear that hate may prove stronger than love. This could result in being harmed or in harming the loved object. Many of these patients need to reality test the fear that their destructiveness is omnipotent. Borderlines have difficulties in maintaining a relationship once it is invaded by conflicts or frustrations. Many of the intensely destructive impulses cannot be expressed. In addition to instability of relationships there are mood fluctuations and identity problems. Common complaints are boredom and intense loneliness. There can be great and pervasive anger, and an overall vulnerability or fragility. Substance abuse, depressive episodes, and transient psychoses may be manifest. There are concerns with power, massive splitting, defenses against disintegration, and feelings of not being entitled to exist. Early maternal deprivation leads to a lack of Eros. Power themes play an important role in therapy with borderlines because of the lack of Eros. The overwhelming fears are of separation, abandonment, and annihilation. Borderlines mistrust and lack the capacity to trust. In some individuals the compensatory sense of entitlement, grandiosity, and the notion that the world owes them a living can be exorbitant.

With some borderline cases there is a transgression of the hypothetical line from the neuroses to the psychoses. With others there is a relatively stable clinical picture in which there are simultaneous signs of psychosis, neurosis, and adequate ego functioning. The wide spectrum of borderline states possesses a varying psychology. Jung's description of the *abaissement* coincides with these patterns of borderline behavior.

As the borderline is close to or lost in the archetypal world, he may experience the archetypal content bursting through easily, as, for example, in the compulsive behavior of the Don Juan. Jung attributes this tendency to a disturbance of the primal relationship at the stage of development when the ego is not yet consolidated. The weakening of the ego makes possible a direct inundation of unconscious contents, which has a restrictive influence on the personality as a whole. Later, the disturbance is reflected in feelings of being forsaken, inferior, uninvolved, and in sadomasochistic reactions. In essence, the primary preoccupation of the borderline is with problems centering on symbiosis and object relatedness.

As archetypes are released and activated by an actual personal encounter with a human being, an adverse emotional experience in relation to the parents, or initially the mother, is a trauma that is responded to with fear, anxiety, aggression, or despair. The child feels overwhelmed by internal forces, unconscious material, and a loss of connection to the totality of the Self. The Self is initially experienced by projection onto the parents. The loss of the mother is experienced as the loss of the ideal state of the Self. The process of development during the first three years is centered on the evocation and differentiation of the archetypes that determine the various components of the child's personality.

The Self is the central archetype and surrounds and contains all the other archetypal elements. Since the Self containing these components of the personality develops within the context of the maternal matrix, and the primary mothering person is viewed as the mediator of the organization of the psyche, the consistent and predictable presence of the good-enough mother throughout the early months of life serves to tie the infant's universe of experience in a particular way. The interrelation between infant and caring mother as a unit becomes the first and most important object relationship. First of all, she prevents traumatic states that overwhelm the infant and impede psychic organization. Then it is through the mother and her body that impulse, feeling, action, and eventually thought become organized as a part of the self and integrated not only with each other but also with the external reality that the mother represents. When early development within this maternal matrix goes well, the outcome is the achievement of a cohesive, reality-related and object-related self.

Disturbances like separation from the mother, hunger, or ill-ness lead to a disturbance in the evocation of the maternal arche-type. These early problems damage the ego-Self axis and result in the psychological problems of the borderline. M. Fordham (1957) concludes that borderlines have a defective process of deintegration in which the Self nuclei are not stably cohesive. With the experience of trauma and unmet needs, the child's original state of inflation begins to dissolve and a state of alienation results. The child who had good physical care but did not experience positive warmth and the child who had too much attention can both suffer injury to the archetypal image of the parent. According to Neumann (1973):

> The predominance of a negative experience inundates the ego nucle-us, dissolves it or gives it a negative charge, or distress ego. . . . The child's experience of the world, the thou, and the Self bears the imprint of distress or doom. (p. 74)

He goes on to say that the roots of the borderline

> are in unfolding of the relations between ego and thou, between ego and body, and between ego and Self, which in the primal relationships are inextricably bound together. . . . The sickness or health of the individual, and his success or failure in later life, are dependent on this process. (p. 44)

The mother carries the projections of the archetype of the Great Mother, or the all-powerful numinious woman on whom one is dependent. The relationship between mother and child is paral-leled by the interaction of the Divine Child and Great Mother in the inner world. Jung (1912, par. 431), in his chapter on "The Battle for Deliverance from the Mother," describes an infantile disposition that is

> always characterized by a predominance of the parental imago . . . because he has freed himself insufficiently, or not at all, from his childish environment. . . . He is incapable of living his own life.

Part of the borderline's personality has achieved a greater level of maturation in interpersonal relatedness. This is the part that initially brings the patient to therapy. Other parts are stuck at the level of symbiosis, where early archetypal constellations or parental introjects have become solidified. This results in impasses and stultification in the development of archetypal patterns. Von Franz (1970), in her study of the *puer aeternus*, notes this mother-bound state of unsconsciouness.

Jung (1953, par. 81) stresses the importance of remembering and reexperiencing the events of childhood, since fragments of childhood need to be integrated into adult consciousness: "The journey with father and mother up and down many ladders represents the making conscious of infantile contents that have not yet been integrated."

The healing of the self can only take place after both analyst and analysand accept the heroic and divine aspects of the child archetype. This leads to a more unified and stable sense of identity. Until this transpires, the analysands cannot really be themselves, or, to paraphrase Winnicott (1965), their true selves. Winnicott regards feeling real as an essential manifestation of the "true self," whereas feeling unreal is a typical propensity of the "false self." Khan (1974) notes that the self is protected from annihilation by staying dissociated and hidden.

Therapy provides an opportunity to repair or reconstruct the injury in the borderline's disorder between ego and self and self and other. According to Lambert (1981), early childhood can be analyzed "both for the repair of damage with a subsequent release of held up development, and to enable the patient to link up emotionally both with his childhood, and . . . in a more realistic way with the Divine Child Archetype" (p. 11). The personal parents need to be differentiated from the archetypal parents. The borderline can be caught up in hate and rebellion toward the parents while at the same idealizing them. The holding environment of the transference/countertransference creates the necessary inner space for "the delusion of oneness between analyst and analysand" (Lambert 1981, p. 12).

The transference/countertransference, as the sine qua non for analytic work, is the vital ingredient in repairing arrests in development and completing the unfinished business of childhood. It also ushers in the newly unfolding or developing aspects of the psyche and furthers the searches for new beginnings and new solutions in the inborn striving for wholeness. Through the use of the transference/countertransference we gain an increased understanding of the interaction between the personal history of the individual and his archetypal development. The transference/countertransference provides the arena for the resolution of the borderline state by reconstituting the transitional space of a *participation mystique* or more symbiotic way of being that allows this healing to take place. The analyst carries the projection of the Self and is identified with

the symbol of a transcendent aim or goal. The painful inner problems of the patient are introjected through the syntonic countertransference. The analyst helps the patient to understand and integrate the material in a new way. This new integration eventually
results in the growth that allows for the patient's independence.
There has been a restoration of contact with the inner sources of
strength and acceptance. The injured image is replaced by an image
of wholeness through the projection of the parental image on the
analyst. According to Jung (1955, par. 232), "What has been spoiled
by the father can only be made good by a father, and what has been
spoiled by the mother can only be repaired by a mother." Only
when an individual has had the experience of a positive relation to
a parental figure can he be released from the negative and destructive aspect holding him in bondage.

Since borderline patients exhibit shaky interpersonal relationships, inability to love, deficiencies in empathy, egocentric perceptions of reality, and solipsistic claims for attention, their behaviors
can erode the therapist's sense of self, making it hard to be a "good-
enough therapist." A good-enough therapist is a sort of combination
of Winnicott's "good-enough mother" and the Jungian ideal of
being in touch with the positive mother complex. The therapist
needs to be empathically in touch with the patient in a way that
offers the opportunity to repair the early damage.

Of course one cannot change the patient's world or undo the
prior unfortunate events. One does not redo the whole person in
therapy. We cannot reconstruct the earlier period of life in the
course of treatment. What we can do is to try and see the elements
of its influence and offer the opportunity for a different kind of
experience. The origins of the problem are secondary to what we
can do about failures in nurturance or development. The basic
questions are what is the person now, how did he or she get that
way, and what can I do in the here and now to help him or her grow
optimally?

One might question the elevation of the concept of transfer-
ence/countertransference to such developmental preeminence.
Some of the questions we can ask are the following:

1. Do we limit the transference/countertransference to distortions or projections that require correction, or can we view it as an
articulation of a perception of an inner perspective or view?

2. Is the transference/countertransference in the past or in the
present?

3. Is the transference/countertransference to be relinquished or is it a part of the individuation process and, as such, part of the life cycle?

4. Is the transference/countertransference an intrapsychic phenomenon, or is it also an external or interpersonal phenomenon?

Jung (1946) answers these questions in "The Psychology of the Transference" when he refers to the crucial experience of the transference in every analysis. He makes the following significant qualifying comments: "The psychotherapist has to acquaint himself not only with the personal biography of his patient, but also with the mental and spiritual assumptions prevalent in his milieu, both present and past, where traditional and cultural influences play a part and often a decisive one" (p. viii). "The transference phenomenon is without doubt one of the most important syndromes in the process of individuation; its wealth of meanings goes far beyond mere personal likes and dislikes. By virtue of its collective contents and symbols, it transcends the individual personality and extends into the social sphere" (par. 539).

I would like to postulate that transference/countertransference, with its basis in projection and introjection, is a universal phenomenon present in early life experiences. Its value for the treatment of the borderline lies therein. Analytic treatment does not create transference/countertransference but only brings it to life, for it is shaped by contemporary external reality in conjunction with inner phenomena. There is no interpersonal life that is separate from intrapsychic life. All transference responses are responses to contemporary events and may be realistic or nonrealistic, adaptive or maladaptive. All of life is transferentially determined by unconscious factors. Any human interaction involves the intrapsychic. The words *intrapsychic* and *interpersonal* have unfortunately degenerated into slogans or buzz words, and the adherents of each approach attack the other. But like the nature versus nurture controversy, both are important.

In fact, there are three states of being: (a) an inner psychic reality that is the personal experience of each individual, (b) an external reality, and (c) an intermediate area combining the experience of the individual and his environment. Inner reality basically contains all of the experiences that we have undergone or have the potential for undergoing, colored by the immature cognitive processes of childhood and by later distortions of the personality. Some are remembered directly, others become inaccessible to recall, and yet others shape the way experiences are processed. The human psyche is an internal world of a personal nature that partly realistically and partly in highly distorted ways reproduces internal relationships in the external world.

The space of the transference/countertransference is similar to the area of illusion. What is objectively perceived and subjectively conceived takes place here. It is the transitional space in between, neither inside nor outside, where we recreate what was originally the facilitating environment for the infant. The essential feature of this space is its illusory character. Given adequate opportunity to participate in the illusion of symbiosis in therapy, the individual can renegotiate separation-individuation and be well on the road to further individuation.

A lack of the capacity to form a therapeutic alliance can reflect an impairment in transference capacity. Sometimes the borderline aspect only becomes manifest after a period of treatment during which the transference/countertransference phenomenon reveals evidence of splitting and denial. Or one notices that the patient has a capacity for slipping in and out of psychotic states or uses psychotic defenses. Simultaneously, there is a fear of the unconscious, of states of fragmentation, and of depersonalization. Borderlines have often not reached the stage of mirroring or idealizing relationships. The transference shows us how personal reality is constructed. It is not in contrast to reality but is a part of it. It provides the opportunity to go into the symptom or sickness and transform the *massa confusa* by connecting with the symbolic meaning of the symptom.

One of the shortcomings of the Jungian approach, except for the contributions of Neumann (1973), Edinger (1972), and M. Fordham (1957), is the lack of an adequate cohesive developmental theory. The analytical process is in itself a developmental process. The application of the findings of infant and child observation, along with object relations theory, to the clinical understanding of adults has contributed to our understanding of stages of transference/countertransference phenomena. The developmental approach to the treatment of the borderline patient allows for the evaluation of changes in intrapsychic structure and psychodynamic functioning. Winnicott (1965) states that he had the unique opportunity to observe infants by noting the specific transference relationships of his severely disturbed patients. F. Fordham (1969, p. 3) noted that "by paying attention to a patient's infancy, one can discover the flaws in his environment which distorted his later development, led to a weak ego structure, and consequent excessive influence of the archetypes." There is something to be said for recommending that all therapists have some experience working with infants and young children and a knowledge of phase-specific development. We need to incorporate knowledge of growth and development in childhood to further our knowledge of normal and pathological developmental processes. In general, the higher the developmental phase attained, the more likely experiences will be expressed in verbal introspections. The lower the developmental phase, the greater likelihood of enactions involving the therapist. Persons emotionally stuck communicate in ways that differ from persons who can differentiate self and other. The borderline has difficulty with symbolizing and basically remains in a world of concrete thinking.

In a previous article (Machtiger 1982), I discussed the role of the transference/countertransference in the healing process. The *unio mystica* of the transitional space allows for the merging and fusing of the harmonious penetrating mix-up that is part of the borderline state. In the blurring of boundaries the gulf is bridged, and the analyst can incarnate earlier parental figures. The therapeutic field facilitates the emergence of a symbiotic situation that is necessary for the release of the archetypal images, and the emergence of the helpful mother imago brings about a new orientation. These experiences have nothing to do with role playing on the part of the analyst but represent an authentic responsiveness to the patient. The projective identification serves a necessary function as it lies at the root of psychic transformation. It is the analyst's ability to eventually show the patient the role that the latter has assigned to him in the transference, and the genesis of this assignment, that carries the potentiality for change. What we construct in clinical work is a myth of genesis, which is not identical to the data of historical development. Therapeutic growth results from the therapist's ability to understand and respond to the patient in a developmentally appropriate way. In other words, how one listens and responds is more important than what one does. Growth is not dependent upon clever interpretations but upon the analyst's constellating and mediating the image of the good parent or healer, or Self, and containing it within the transference/countertransference. Borderlines require a compelling interpersonal involvement.

While each transference/countertransference is unique, certain realities of the analytic situation can be used to build up the psychic unity between analyst and analysand. The temenos, or maturationally facilitative matrix, is created by the room, the hour, and being part of each other's lives. It is a shared interaction. The analyst makes a commitment to feel for, about, and with the patient while maintaining the necessary separateness. Jung (1946) notes that the success or failure of treatment is bound up with the transference in a very fundamental way.

Borderline patients can become hypercritical about their treatment and their therapists. They are constantly seeking ammunition for their rage and are marvelous at ferreting out the therapist's Achilles' heel in their need to provoke and manipulate. There is a need to experience the therapist as hostile and controlling; the patient's paranoia and bitterness can thus be justified. While distrusting and fearing the therapist, borderlines simultaneously try to appease and placate. Any perceived deficiency in empathy becomes a cause célèbre and is reacted to with disappointment and rage.

In the literature on borderline syndromes, it is recognized that one of the difficulties with borderlines is their ability to create a confused state in the analyst. By projecting their self-hatred onto the analyst, they can succeed in paralyzing him or her. Since the transferences can be more chaotic and archaic and are fraught with projective identification, many borderlines require more of a here and now handling and sometimes a more confrontative mode.

In the early stages of the transference/countertransference the therapist is not experienced as a separate person but as a transitional object. The patient cannot begin new growth until the therapist finds a way to replicate the original form of symbiotic relatedness. Loss or separation from the symbiotic partner remains the key in borderline personality disorders. If the process is allowed to develop, eventually an internalization of the images can take place and there is a greater differentiation of self and object. Misperceptions and misconstructions of self/object relations can take place and be explored in the constancy of the dynamic process of the analytic relationship. The fragmented self of the patient merges with the "Rock of Gibraltar" therapist and borrows from the therapist what could not be obtained in childhood. There are some patients who need to do this in a surreptitious way, and any evidence of progress or feeling better is hidden. This can engender self-doubt, incompetence, impotence, and defeat in the analyst, feelings often related to the feelings of emptiness inside the patient. The analyst's boredom might point out an affective absence on the part of the patient.

The transference/countertransference keeps changing during the course of therapy. At the outset of treatment, the symbiosis is allowed to develop, since the transference reactions of borderlines have their roots in the developmental state prior to the interpersonal experience of whole objects. The interaction in this cocoonlike *participation mystique,* in this symbiotic state of the transference/ countertransference, is therapeutic since oneness facilitates the elicitation of affects and archetypal images surrounding unconscious fantasies, memories, and images that can be held, differentiated, and ultimately integrated into a symbolic form.

The two patients I discuss in this paper have failed to achieve a high level of differentiating self from other, although differentiation in its earlier and more primitive stages had been accomplished. There was a failure to integrate good and bad aspects of experience in accordance with the increasing perceptual and cognitive abilities of the child. This resulted in a persistent proneness to identity disorganization.

As the borderline is unable to appreciate the other as psychically independent of his own needs and interests, there is a tendency to anticipate a consistent attitude of maternal preoccupation from important relationships. Merger fantasies in the transference often reflect primitive fusions from the deepest levels of symbiosis. The patients with better reality testing find this an intolerable state of being and equate the loss of identity with going crazy. In this state, there is a tendency to withdraw interest from the other person by denigrating the other.

In actual relationships, the borderline patient oscillates between painful detachment and frightening overinvolvement. Some may find separateness frightening on the basis of their excessive idealization of the analyst, with consequent excessive dependence not threatening to their psychic existence. The fear of possible abandonment is the threat. In the treatment situation, the transference reflects the failure of full differentiation. The terror at separation is particularly evident at the times before vacations and holidays. Some of these patients need to be seen by somebody else, while others come down with bodily illness, decompensate, or act out various kinds of self-injury. They may take up dangerous personal relationships or use drugs and alcohol to excess. There may be an increased number of cancellations before or after a long holiday. Patients who utilize denial are more apt to show this reaction. Some may actually act out manic behavior. With these patients, the achievement of missing the analyst or grieving for the loss is often a major breakthrough. There is a realization that separation can occur without aggression, retaliation, or being abandoned by the other person. One can relinquish a measure of control and allow the other person an independent existence. It does not lead to a complete loss of control, chaos, or finding oneself in the other person's power.

The transference of the borderline bears similarities to the narcissistic transference in which the analyst is not experienced as a whole, separate person but rather as an extension of the needs of the patient. The analyst is needed to maintain the patient's self-esteem. There is excessive projection and a distorted evaluation of the external world. Empathy is shallow, anxiety tolerance impaired, and the capacity for concern and mourning limited and impoverished. There is a greater likelihood of an *abaissement du niveau mental* under stress.

The therapy of the patients I discuss here fits the descriptive material previously presented. There were boundary problems, questions of sexual identity, and initial issues of substance abuse. Although the primary focus of attention was on transference/countertransference, initially the patients' communications of developmental and transferential expressions were not interpreted. The patients' problems with the self started with maladaptive environmental care. Premature confrontations and interpretations would be maladaptive too and are therefore to be avoided while one is holding the patient in the area of illusion. Certain experiences can then become actualized, and transformations can take place. The main task is to learn how to function in such a way with the patient as to correct or reverse some of the earlier experiences. Jung (1946) believed that "the patient needs you in order to unite his dissociated personality in your unity, calm and security."

The first phase of treatment was similar to the treatment of any serious personality disorder. The basic aim was to create the empathic environment in which trust could grow and affect be ventilated. With the replication of the symbiosis, differentiation of affects such as rage and envy could emerge. The analyst's task is to mediate between the opposites and keep the patient from falling apart. During this phase there is often regressive behavior. Episodes of confusion, fragmenting, and emotional flooding often usher in new levels of integration. The conflict was rooted in the giving up of the symbiotic partnership or earlier state for a more differentiated one. This reorganizing process could then move the person forward.

Case History: Mr. C

Mr. C. was a 34-year-old man in the early stages of a professional scientific career who began twice-weekly treatment shortly after finishing a doctorate and moving away from the geographic location of his family of origin. In outward appearance C seemed fairly well integrated. He had done well academically, professionally, and, it seemed from externals, socially. Under the surface there was a limited range of absolutely fixed ideas belonging to a very early level of development. C was a man who feared and hated his own immaturity and weakness in the face of everyday living and in comparison with other people. His marriage had been stressful from the beginning and involved sexual problems and episodes of wife beating. His wife, in an effort to extricate herself from the marriage of 10 years, accepted a job in another city.

There were also work-related problems with peers and feelings of being overwhelmed by the new job. C described himself as being on the thin edge of exhaustion, drinking too much, using drugs, and feeling he was on trial in the work situation and being crucified by his superiors. Suicidal ideation and hypochondriacal concerns were present. A weak psychosomatic integration made him liable to psychosomatic illness. C insisted that illness is either entirely somatic or entirely psychogenic. Psyche and soma had to be kept apart. In his early history, there was a pronounced lack of early bodily closeness that would have enriched the buildup of psychosomatic unity. Concerns with sexual adequacy led him to overcompensate in the realm of educational and intellectual endeavor. He could achieve this by getting into a martyr complex. The Adlerian concept of organ inferiority is an apt description of his modus operandi.

In our first meeting I was informed that C was an Aristotelian who did not like to look at motives or get involved in "psychobabble." The religious function was repressed and he was an atheist. After sharing an initial dream of trying to tend to a young man with a hole in his head, he expressed fear that I would be like lace, too fragile and needing his protection, or that I'd be taken in by his bullshit.

When I was with him early in therapy, it felt as if he never lived far from the edge of explosive physical violence. There was a virtual reservoir of repressed and suppressed rage. Sessions were punctuated by abusive, angry outbursts. The first few times that this rage erupted in a session, he got very upset. After the first occasion, he presented me with a bouquet of flowers, saying he felt stupid and embarrassed, yet he knew that he really did not have to apologize to me. After the second episode, he wrote a note of apology, not so much as an act of reparation but as an insurance policy to forestall rejection. Some of these outbursts felt like brief paranoidal experiences. These mini-psychotic episodes were short lived and continued to appear at times of temporary intense anxiety and stress.

In the initial sessions there was nothing but positive regard for his mother. As things progressed, he mentioned in passing that she had been hospitalized with severe depression for the nine months following his birth. He felt that his birth had damaged her. His mother returned to work as a child librarian at the local school before he was three years of age. Despite her career, she had fixed notions about men's and women's work in the home. Men did not participate in household chores. His father would return from work and drink himself into semi-oblivion while his mother prepared dinner. His father was depicted as short tempered, often crude, and frequently drunk. At times he would stagger in the door, reeking of alcohol, and sprawl out on the livingroom floor. Several times he lost his balance and, in a bloody state of unconsciousness, urinated on the floor. C would clean his father's wounds and drag him off to bed. In the morning it was as though the incident had never occurred. Early on in therapy he could not recall having felt anything, nor could he remember his mother's reaction. It was only midway through therapy that he was able to feel the terror and pain and could weep when talking about his early life.

His mother was portrayed as a quiet, unassuming, and gentle woman who espoused the myth that women were too weak to cope with the rigors of life. Simultaneously, she was strong willed, quite tough, and much shrewder financially than her husband. C viewed her as the queen bee who dispenses with the male once she is impregnated. Early on in therapy, he dreamed of a man tearing a rear wall out of building in order to rescue a queen bee and place it in an enclosure in the front of his childhood home. In another dream he was protecting this home from a 14-foot tiger lurking outside. He had a small pistol which was useless against the tiger. The dream of the 14-foot tiger was followed by a dream of a little dog eating the tail of a big cat. The associations were to early memories of believing that his mother had a phallus.

There was a recollection of an incident at age eight when he felt his parents were not in touch with his feelings. After injuring a foot playing outdoors he came in the door trailing blood. He was scolded and punished for making a fuss and mess. The blood had to be cleaned up before medical attention was sought.

The relationship with a sister three years his senior was highly ambivalent. They had engaged in exploratory sex play, and he later used her bed for masturbation. There was jealousy, as he saw her as the more favored and gifted child. Several years ago he purchased brother and sister kittens and allowed them to have a litter before having them neutered. This material paved the way for an exploration of his sexuality. There were dreams of homosexual encounters under heterosexual cover-up and a dream of his sister turning into a demonic-faced man while in bed with him. In another dream, a male was swimming on the surface of the water while a female was making porpoiselike movements underneath.

The archetypal constellation was of someone caught in the grips of homosexuality. C was like one of Gaia's children: a child trapped in the earth. As long as his masculinity was embedded in the maternal matrix, he was unable to genuinely utilize his ego in an assertive way. In his regressive pull toward the unconscious, C could not contact the masculine qualities that would result in the assumption of more assertive behavior. Until this was possible, C had to seek it out in other people and incorporate it in a magical way.

As therapy continued, he complained of feeling increasingly isolated, lonely, and distrustful and he found it hard to tolerate other people. He would find himself denigrating others so as to feel superior. It soon became clear that there were chronic feelings of anger, deprivation, and disappointment at what was experienced as a lack of concern and attention on my part. Failure to attend to him was experienced as not only done to him, but because of him. There were also difficulties in impulse control.

When homosexual and transsexual themes came up, he experienced vertigo, tremor, and nausea. During the work day and on business trips, he was terrified of becoming sexually aroused toward male colleagues. Colleagues at work were perceived as making obvious but unconscious homosexual displays toward him. In addition to dealing with his homosexual feelings through projective identification, C would periodically resort to masturbation accompanied by primitive merger themes and sadomasochistic activity. Business trips were particularly traumatic, especially when he was expected to share a room with a colleague. There were numerous panic attacks, and he decompensated. At those times he would ask the men to hold him and comfort him. The desire was to be held, cared for, and nurtured. What was needed was not a particular person but a state of being, of unhurtness, and containment.

With an overall restlessness, incapacity for relaxation, and agitation, a strong sense of tension was ever present. Desperate feelings surfaced when there was no one to offer a sustaining relationship. There were fears of separation, clinging states, and a terror of being invaded and possessed. Since survival was bound up in and dependent upon another person, the threat of annihilation was ever present. Eventually, my task was to help him piece together by genetic reconstruction all the bits and pieces of his early life and relate them to his feelings for me. It was as though he were hearing it for the first time. This part of the work helped him differentiate between the real mother and the archetypal mother. It was only after I had become a new object of identification by carrying the incarnation of the mother archetype and constellating an alternate parental image in the unconscious that C was able to tolerate criticism of the symbiotic parent. Previously, when he would bestow upon me the numinious power of the Great Mother, there was a tremendous pull to remain in the world of fantasy. When ego and consciousness were more developed, I became the bad mother on whom he could courageously unleash all his negative feelings as he struggled to separate the objective reality of the personal mother from the archetype of the Great Mother. Sometimes I was the critical mother who could never be satisfied. At other times I was a kind of Circe, who magically knew what was going on inside him and was out to enchant and capture him.

C saw me as having two personalities. My predominant mode was a mean and calculating one. The reason for my becoming an analyst was that it gave me an opportunity to indulge to the utmost all of my sadistic fantasies. I knew how to frustrate him by determining precisely what he wanted from me, and then by not acceding to these desires I could torture him with great glee. Manipulation was also my forte. Sometimes I commented that these qualities resembled some of his own and amplified my comments with descriptions of our interactions. He would then be reflective. At other times I would not confront him with reasonableness or reality. On rare occasions I was seen as helpful and caring. The problem was that what he perceived of as my alternating personalities made me totally unpredictable.

An ever-present and prominent theme in the transference/countertransference was his attempt to inveigle me into his sadomasochistic life pattern. He could not openly ask for help because he was not able to tolerate the thought of a possible refusal without being consumed by hostile fantasies or fears of abandonment. This transferential aspect was rooted in the earlier experience of parental rejection. C had learned that it was futile to have expectations of others. In this masochistic pattern, the transference feeling is that the therapist will be rejecting too. My countertransference was of being in a tenuous position, with feelings of frustration and impotence. At times my inability to comprehend the dynamics of what might be going on left me discouraged and depressed. At other times, he would goad me and try to provoke an angry reaction. When intensely angry he would tell me that the "Jack the Ripper" aspect was coming close to the surface. It was described as fiery underneath with water dashing against the rocks and creating steam.

On numerous occasions he would accuse me of not responding to his need for help. This need surfaced in somatic complaints or in requests to do something for him that would help him get his wife back. I was the mother who was indifferent to his pain, and even if I took note of it, I was too incompetent to do anything about it.

In the transference, we went from my being an impersonal, inhuman, computer-technician-type of professional whom he experienced as virtually nonexistent, to my being a seductive siren. There was a badgering to meet with him outside of sessions. If I refused to do so, he said he was doomed to bachelorhood. In the midst of these pleas, he said he could not get involved with another woman "until he finished with" me. When he expressed warm, erotic feelings toward me, he would appear ashamed and embarrassed. I assented to his difficulty and allowed him to continue. When he looked away I would say, "you look uncomfortable," but would not make any premature interpretations that would analyze the feelings away. At the time, he dreamed of some men who were trying to stem the flow of red-hot lava in the basement. The lava started to emerge out of the opening and he was helping to plug the flow by throwing whatever he could get his hands on into the opening.

The anger at my not always being there when he wanted me to be, as well as my not having a sexual relationship with him, abated somewhat after he had an image of running over a short wooden bridge. "I'm running toward a woman dressed in a loose white gown. She has black hair tumbling down to her shoulders. Her arms may be slightly raised toward me. She is disturbingly familiar, but I cannot place the resemblance. Certainly, none of the obvious people I can think of. That's all I get, but it's compelling somehow." The woman turned out to resemble his youthful mother. As he grieved for what he had missed in childhood, C realized that what he wanted was not physical closeness with me in the here and now but the closeness of the infant with the mother's body.

The rage-filled baby occupied a large part of the therapy. We needed to bring this traumatized infant into communication with C. He worked through much psychic pain. The fact that I was a separate individual with needs and wishes not coinciding with his was excruciatingly painful. Until the rage was recognized and integrated he would feel unlovable. The terror of the rage, and the pain, needed to be heard.

It was difficult to remain in a state of syntonic countertransference. Positive responses were experienced as gratifications; negative responses were my wanting him to suffer. His responses were that of the young child whose elated and depleted states are connected to feeding experiences and awareness of its own body.

C complained about my inadequacies as a therapist, the inequality of the treatment situation, the demeaning of the patient, and how this therapy was going nowhere. My response to all this was to ask questions and to listen. Mr. C was externalizing his own difficulties and disappointments and making me the deficient child self. He could then be the critical, sadistic parent and attack me. It was crucial for me to survive the psychonoxious effects in good health. In this way, C was better able to gain acceptance of his own needy child. When feeling dominated by this child, I would need to resist reacting by blaming, attacking, or appeasing C. This would lead to feelings of fatigue, depression, and at times even detachment. When I could feel pain again, it was an alternative to feeling nothing. At those times, C would say I was useless.

Sometimes in the transference there was anger at my underestimating his ability. Particularly when he was experiencing grandiosity, my role was to be a one-person combination of mirror, pep squad, and admiration society to cheer him on to even greater feats. If I did not do this, I became the mother who wanted to keep him nonfunctional. At other times he complained that I was pushing too hard. Then I was rated as the kind of therapist who needed to put people down in order to feel more important. Anything I said was denied, derided, or destroyed. C would get impaled and wallow in the role of the suffering victim. The pressure for rescue was unrelenting; after all, I was responsible for his welfare. After a period of immersion in this theme, he had a dream of getting in the driver's seat of a car and refusing to use his mother's road map. This was followed by a dream in which his mother abandoned him. I was there telling his mother that she didn't understand how C really felt. In the sessions, he expressed anger at me for not allowing his functional part to come out. He was not accomplishing anything because I did not have expectations.

In the transference he was struggling with two images of the self: an omnipotent, grandiose one, which was equated with being functional, and a contemptible one, which was nonfunctional. Where there was a push to be dependent, C would say he was falling apart and needed to be hospitalized. The idea that there was no one to offer him a sustaining relationship panicked him, and he felt then that I should care for him. He dreamed that he could not get a job promotion until he had finished nursery school.

There was a shift in the transference/countertransference from hating himself for not achieving to hating me for holding him back. This switch, ironically, provided the impetus for growth. The issue of what is therapeutically useful is enormously important, complicated, and controversial. At times it was tempting to confront C with the contradictory nature of his transference reactions. On the rare occasion when this happened, we ended up in a confusing morass. When I attempted to clarify my original formulation, I ended up forgetting my original point.

If I talked about his difficulties, he felt criticized. Everything said was a painful reminder of my superior creative power, which then needed to be nullified. What seemed to help him most was for me to accept all that he had to say about me, particularly the negative things. In doing so, the analytic setting provided a safe place, or temenos, for both the positive and negative feelings. The image of me as both good and bad, strong and weak, began to come together.

Another area of important work was the gradual acceptance of my not making decisions for him or pushing him to get better. There were many complaints of my being a cold, uninvolved, unfeeling bitch. Ultimately he realized that this coldness meant that I was not going to control him. This led to fewer fears of loss of identity and autonomy. Eventually there was an awareness that his concern about being taken over was rooted in his own wish to do so to others. C was more aware of the infantile part of himself that undermined his more adult side by remaining in the grips of the *puer aeternus* archetype.

Case History: Ms. S.

Ms. S, a 26-year-old divorced woman, began four-times-a-week therapy after being referred by the local mental health facility. Her

illness became manifest during adolescence; her first hospitalization was when she was 16, although there were numerous hospital-
izations for illness in early childhood. She was the youngest of six
children, two of whom died before she was born. The family constellation was a rather complicated one. The patient's mother was
the result of a casual liaison and had been sent to live in foster
homes for 14 years. She was then brought back to live with her own
mother and her mother's common-law husband in a ménage à trois.
This man fathered S and the other five children. When S was three-
and-a-half, her 64-year-old father died of a malignancy of the larynx.
S found him dead on the lavatory floor.

S looked much younger than her actual years and had an aura
of fragility about her. In our early sessions, she denied having any
major problems, past or present, and described herself as being too
detached and unable to get close to people to form relationships,
even with "friends." Pervasive feelings of emptiness and depression
were ever present, along with a sense of unreality.

The initial transference was a negative one. The night before
our first meeting she dreamed that she went to see a stern therapist
who made her feel trapped. That feeling stayed with her all day. As
she saw it, therapists were in it for the money, or because of their
own problems, which included needing to be in a position of power
over others. She did not want a mad Jungian who was more messed
up than she was. She was afraid that if she became involved with
me, I would take over and she would cease to exist. She viewed
analysis as brain washing, and if she did not fight my attempts at
brainwashing, I could take over. She felt that it was abnormal to
trust people, and she asked me to confirm this view of life. She did
not like me and would make sure that she did not need me. Her
motivation for continuing to see me was that she could not understand the intensity of her anger toward me.

S was quite gifted in being able to portray accurately her inner
state, and the typical problems of the borderline can be well illus-
trated in the content of her material. For the first few months she
kept me uninformed about the circumstances of her everyday life,
as well as her past history, but they came tumbling out as she began
to trust me. There was a need to maintain a dissociation between
external life and fantasy life. The message conveyed was "keep
away." There was an interesting combination of arrogance and
inferiority with a suggestion of having to defend herself against any
external supplier of self-esteem and any dependency feelings. S
described herself as having two opposite parts: One, which she

named her Irish part, was a megalomaniac who thought she could do anything and everything and could talk to anyone; the other, inferior part was the recipient of contempt for her weakness, helplessness, and dependence.

Some of the time S would be in a typical depressive state, complaining of insomnia, anorexia, withdrawal from social contacts, bombarding herself with accusations, particularly with respect to irritability and hostility toward her children. At other times she appeared disconnected, confused, and nonresponsive, and showed signs of depersonalization. She would describe herself as being dead, not here, encapsulated in a bubble, covered with cotton, or separated from me by a sheet of glass. During these disturbances in sensation, self-perception, and communication, S would often ask if I could see her. At times I would hold her hand. It was important for me to be there and to share her terrified state with her.

A persistent problem was her inability to handle envious and destructive feelings toward me. When she was absorbed with anxiety and guilt over these feelings, it was difficult for her to maintain contact with me. At the same time there was the inability to tolerate the feeling of separateness from me. She would shut me out and then feel cut off, and she would panic. Periodically S had to make sure her angry feelings had not damaged me and would ask, "Are you all right?" or "Are you there?"

In our relationship, S was trying to achieve union with the idealized object. She had to avoid the feelings of separateness as she used our relationship to work out the problems rooted in her early life. Our relationship represented the fusion between self and object images based on primitive mechanisms of projection and introjection. My role was to be Winnicott's "good-enough mother" and to allow her to communicate her sense of anger toward her mother and her feelings of desolation about her father's death and her grandmother's deliberate withdrawal from the family. As our relationship deepened and we established more trust, S began to let me into her inner world, which was populated with voices. It took two years of meeting from four to seven times a week before she could share that she lived in two worlds and did not belong to the real world. There were auditory and visual hallucinations. The blurred-faced people included a wise and frightening old man, an ogre type, a snivelling child, and a black man. She labeled the figures "The Mafia" and had known since childhood that she belonged to them and that they would eventually claim her. Meanwhile she struggled not to be taken over. The clash of the two realities was seen as ending in her annihilation. The more she trusted me, the more prominent the voices became. We shared the struggle with the voices who were telling her that therapy was useless. Periodically she would go through a phase of accusing me of being the smartest con of all, the chief agent of this Mafia, her biggest enemy.

She took to hiding under a blanket. One day, when I said she must be very lonesome, a hand came out from under the blanket. I grasped the hand and she started to sob. Before she left she asked if she could take the blanket with her. It became her transitional object. She told me that she had loved a blanket as a small child. Her mother had taken the blanket and washed it; S had tried to reach the wet blanket but could not. She never saw the blanket again.

For a long time she could not accept the Mafia as split-off parts of herself, but as she became able to accept her own rage and angry feelings, the power of the voices abated.

There was one hospitalization during the therapy. Prior to the admission, S had a series of dreams centering around hospitals; this was in contradiction to her conscious attitude where she denied being ill. There were also dreams of water coming up through floorboards, babies with hydrocephalic heads, bombed-out buildings, crashed airplanes, and children smearing themselves with feces. Shortly after her hospital admission she had two dreams conveying her psychic state. In the first she was in a canoe and saw a big tidal wave coming. It was August 6th, the day of Hiroshima, and she could not get out of the way. She knew that in radiation sickness her skin would come off and she would be on fire with her skin bursting. In the second dream she was in a pond full of crocodiles at night. Terrified, she saw a ladder leading up into a tree but was not sure she could make it up to safety.

Although the hospitalization looked like an alarming regression, it was more of a *reculer pour mieux sauter* or what Jung (1946) describes as an amassing and integration of powers that will develop into a new order. S was swamped by the emergence of strong, infantile, rageful feelings. She projected this infant onto me and experienced a psychological rebirth by identifying with this infant. My presence provided the containment and continuity that she needed to experience.

After the hospital stay, S was able to mobilize some positive feelings toward her mother. Two thoughts dominated: either "come here" or "go away." This was identical to what I experienced in the transference/countertransference. She expressed much anger toward her father for having a family late in life and then dying. There was more ability to tolerate painful feelings about the unmet needs of her childhood. There were many sessions when I had to rely on the use of body language, gestures, and actions as analytic material. In the occasions when S felt persecuted by me, she would say that I already knew her thoughts, so they did not have to be verbalized. At other times, when her thinking was inhibited, she would panic at feeling cut off and isolated from me. There was a constant need to be alert to events that would precipitate the regressional and confusional states and, at appropriate times, to use detailed transference interpretations to facilitate the confrontations with the inner psychic contents expressed in her projections.

The grand theme was S's need to damage me and to destroy our relationship and the therapy. In this way she could substantiate her self-hatred, her sense of being evil and unlovable. At the same time it enabled her to triumph over me. It appeared in the fear that one of us must die or commit suicide.

S was an expert at manipulation and would try hard to make me feel guilty, depressed, upset, fed-up, or responsible for her welfare. At times it was extremely difficult to differentiate between her hysterical manipulation and the symptoms of her distress and deep disturbance.

S's poor contact with reality led to my being more open about my feelings. This helped her sort out her feelings from mine. The mode of our relationship and the style of therapy varied with the state of mind of the patient. I found that I had to be very flexible in approach and needed to ascertain what S's capacity for tolerance of anxiety was at a particular time. There were occasions when I had to slip in and out of her psychotic episodes to try to understand what was happening. Together we had to maintain the delicate balance in the fluid relationship between the inner and outer worlds contained in Jung's concept of the *abaissement.*

Summary

As therapy progressed with both of these patients, changes from borderline to higher level functioning took place along the following highly interrelated dimensions.

There was greater cohesiveness of self and object representations, with movement from a more narcissistic to a more interpersonal relatedness. There was more capacity for self-reflection and containment of conflict without acting out. Interaction with people was less fragmented and was no longer of the need-fulfilling part object variety that had made for obvious difficulties in the more adult world. There was less massive projection of unconscious contents and a concurrent greater ability to assume responsibility for contents of the psyche. These patients no longer experienced themselves as weaklings, forever being pushed around. They fought more successfully for the things they felt entitled to. For a while they were afraid of the consequences of being successful and competent.

There were progressive developmental swings between the poles of merger and detachment of the ego-self axis. They described entering relationships with less wish for, less experience of and less defense against merger. They consciously and deliberately tried to limit the frequency of contact, or the speed with which they would be involved, with others and activities. At the same time there was more of a need for others. C used to say, "I don't need anyone. I can be alone as long as I want. I have things to keep me content." Eventually he realized his need for real people and could not be satisfied with evoking images in his mind.

Another milestone in treatment was the ability to share details about decisions and everyday problems. Initially, due to the need to merge, sharing these problems was equated with a loss of ownership of them, which meant I could take credit for them.

The capacity for self-reflection was ushered in by deep depressive reactions to the realization that it was the deepest wishes that made it impossible to maintain relationships with any lasting worth and led to profound loneliness. It was the desire to merge that led to withdrawal in relationships. The depressive reaction corresponded to what Balint (1968) described as the patient's awareness of his or her basic fault—the realization that the difficulties are caused by something wrong in the patient. There is a need to mourn what has been missed and will never transpire. It is the internalization of the positive symbiosis in the transference/countertransference that permits this reaction to take place. These depressive episodes need to be accepted without interference. The old wishes cannot be met; the old ways of coping do not work. This acceptance can result in a move toward more adult functioning. To release themselves from the transference, patients must understand that they no longer need the gratification they once desired and that they must abandon the wish to rectify the old traumatic situation or event. Predominant transference/countertransference patterns of treatment included the all-powerful good mother of early infancy, the mother with whom one longs to merge. Then there was the mother of later infancy and childhood—controlling and intrusive. There was also a hostile and abandoning mother who would abandon them prematurely. Sometimes a powerful, idealized father image would get constellated. At other times, a fused mother–father image arose. To all of these powerful constellations there was a wish to submit, but this wish could be tempered by fear. There were requests for advice and positive guidance. The analyst was requested to be tougher, more confrontive, more demanding, and even to set limits.

There was also a transference through projective identification of an extremely contemptible, useless, helpless, ineffectual part. The contrasting projective identification of the capacity to hope and to improve would also make its presence known. All these transferences were accompanied by intense affect.

The most conspicuous and profound countertransference reaction to all of this was in response to the transference of the denigrated self. It was only after these feelings lessened in the patients and there was less need for me to carry these projections that I was able to experience a tremendous sense of relief. I had come closer to being a whole person because of these patients, and they were more aware of my having been helpful to them at times. They are now strong enough to be able to provide for themselves from their own inner resources.

References

Balint, M. 1968. *The basic fault*. London: Tavistock.
Edinger, E. 1972. *Ego and archetype*. New York: G. P. Putnam's Sons.
Fordham, F. 1969. Some views on individuation. *Journal of Analytical Psychology* 14/1:1–12.
Fordham, M. 1957. Origins of the ego in childhood. In *New developments in analytical psychology*, pp. 104–30. London: Routledge & Kegan Paul.
Franz, M. L. von. 1970. *Puer aeternus*. New York: Spring Publications.
Grinker, R. R., and Dry, R. D. 1968. *The borderline syndrome*. New York: Basic Books.
Harding, E. M. 1965. *The parental image*. New York: G. P. Putnam's Sons.
Jung, C. G. 1912. The battle for deliverance from the mother. In *Collected works*, 5:274–305. Princeton: Princeton University Press, 1956.
_____. 1946. The psychology of the transference. In *Collected works*, 16:163–323. Princeton: Princeton University Press, 1966.
_____. 1953. *Psychology and alchemy*. In *Collected works*, vol. 12. Princeton: Princeton University Press, 1968.
_____. 1955. *Mysterium coniunctionis*. In *Collected works*, vol. 14. Princeton: Princeton University Press, 1970.

Khan, M. 1974. *The privacy of the self.* London: Hogarth.
Knight, R. P. 1954. Borderline states. In *Psychoanalysis, psychiatry and psychology,* pp. 97–109, R. P. Knight and C. R. Friedman, eds. New York: International Universities Press.
Kohut, H. 1971. *Analysis of the self.* New York: International Universities Press.
Lambert, K. 1981. *Analysis, repair and individuation.* London: Academic Press.
Machtiger, H. G. 1982. Countertransference/transference. In *Jungian analysis,* pp. 86–110, M. Stein, ed. La Salle, Ill., and London: Open Court.
Neumann, E. 1973. *The child.* New York: G. P. Putnam's Sons.
Winnicott, D. W. 1965. *The maturational processes and the facilitating environment.* London: Hogarth.

Psychological Types in Transference, Countertransference, and the Therapeutic Interaction

John Beebe

A Model of Psychological Types

The theory of psychological types has failed, I believe, to realize its clinical potential because it has largely been misused. Many Jungian therapists are attracted at first by the theory, with its seductive polarity of extravert and introvert and the promise of wholeness within that elegant quaternity of functions: sensation, thinking, feeling, and intuition. These therapists are led to believe that they can understand their patients simply by labeling them appropriately. At first this method seems to work, but eventually it leads to embarrassing contradictions. For example, a patient diagnosed by his therapist as an introverted intuitive (because he did not seem to do much and vividly reported dreams that were full of imagery) is discovered to be an introverted sensation type, whose extraverted

John Beebe, M.D., is a member of the C. G. Jung Institute of San Francisco, where he is editor of *The San Francisco Jung Institute Library Journal.* A graduate of Harvard College and the University of Chicago Medical School, he did his psychiatric residency at Stanford University Medical Center and his analytic training at the C. G. Jung Institute of San Francisco. He is the editor of *Psychiatric Treatment: Crisis, Clinic, and Consultation* (1975) and *Money, Food, Drink, Fashion, and Analytic Training: Depth Dimensions of Physical Existence* (1983). He has a private practice in San Francisco.

sensation is weak not because it is his inferior function but because it is the shadow function to his superior, introverted sensation. In retrospect, the therapist realizes that he was led to the introverted intuitive diagnosis partly because a previous analyst had assigned it to the patient and partly because the patient, having read Jung, defined himself intuitively in early contacts with the therapist. The therapist is thus forced to admit that he misdiagnosed the patient.

Such experiences lead many therapists to abandon the use of psychological types, joining that large group of analysts in the International Association for Analytical Psychology who do not find the types especially useful in clinical practice (see Plaut 1972). I think that the difficulties involved in using the psychological types with precision are what make them interesting. I have been attempting for some time to formulate a model that will make it possible to use the types with rigor—at least with that degree of rigor Jung calls for in his foreword to the Argentine edition of *Tipos Psicológicos,* which appeared in 1936:

> A psychology that is grounded on experience always touches upon personal and intimate matters and thus arouses everything that is contradictory and unclarified in the human psyche. If one is plunged, as I am for professional reasons, into the chaos of psychological opinions, prejudices, and susceptibilities, one gets a profound and indelible impression of the diversity of individual psychic dispositions, tendencies, and convictions, while on the other hand one increasingly feels the need for some kind of order among the chaotic multiplicity of points of view. This need calls for a critical orientation and for general principles and criteria, not too specific in their formulation, which may serve as *points de repère* ["indications, guiding marks, or landmarks"] in sorting out the empirical material. (Jung 1971, p. xiv)

To satisfy Jung's call, I will have to be more specific in my formulation of the types than Jung himself was. I have found that in the model of psychological types to which Jungian therapists have become accustomed, too much is unclear and too many illogical conclusions have been drawn. For example, someone may be labeled either an extravert or an introvert, as if the extraverted or introverted attitude encompassed all three of that person's leading psychological functions, leaving only the unadapted inferior function to express the whole of the individual's opposing introversion or extraversion. Thus I, for example, am an extravert with intuition as my leading function, and thus it may be assumed that I am also extraverted in my thinking and in my feeling. According to this typological model, my meager introverted sensation, somewhere in the unconscious, is forced to carry the whole of my relation to the inner world. A more democratic model allowing me two extraverted and two introverted functions is only slightly more promising. According to this model, my leading functions, both superior intuition and auxiliary thinking, are both subsumed under my supposedly overarching extraversion, leaving my relatively inferior feeling and absolutely inferior sensation to carry my introversion in an altogether inferior and unadapted way.

I have never been so one-sidedly extraverted as these two models would imply. For many years, some of my friends have been sure that I am introverted, whereas others have been convinced of my dominant extraversion. The reason for this disparity of opinions is that three implications of Jung's typological theory have been overlooked: (a) the constant presence of the auxiliary process, (b) the results of the combinations of perception and judgment, and (c) the role of the auxiliary in balancing extraversion–introversion. Isabel Myers and her mother, Katharine C. Briggs, made Jung's points explicit during their development of that sensitive and widely used instrument, the Myers-Briggs Type Indicator (Briggs and Myers 1979). Myers and Myers (1980, pp. 18–21) quote Jung on these points as follows.

- On the constant presence of the auxiliary:

In conjunction with the most differentiated function, another function of secondary importance, and therefore of inferior differentiation in consciousness, is constantly present, and is a relatively determining factor. (Jung 1923, p. 513; see also Jung 1971, par. 666)

Experience shows that the secondary function is always one whose nature is different from, though not antagonistic to, the leading function: thus, for example, thinking as primary function can readily pair with intuition as auxiliary, or indeed equally well with sensation, but . . . never with feeling. (Jung 1923, p. 515; see also Jung 1971, par. 668)

- On the combinations of perception and judgment:

From these combinations well-known pictures arise, the practical intellect for instance paired with sensation, the speculative intellect breaking through with intuition, the artistic intuition which selects and presents its images by means of feeling judgment, the philosophical intuition which, in league with a vigorous intellect, translates its vision into the sphere of comprehensible thought, and so forth. (Jung 1923, p. 515; see also Jung 1971, par. 669)

- On the role of the auxiliary in balancing extraversion–introversion:

For all the types appearing in practice, the principle holds good that besides the conscious main function there is also a relatively unconscious auxiliary function which is in every respect different from the nature of the main function. (Jung 1923, p. 515; see also Jung 1971, par. 669)

It is from the final quote that Myers has abstracted the principle that I consider to be essential in any discussion of psychological types. According to Myers and Myers (1980, pp. 19, 21):

The basic principle that the auxiliary provides needed extraversion for the introverts and needed introversion for the extraverts is vitally important. The extraverts' auxiliary gives them access to their own inner life and to the world of ideas; the introverts' auxiliary gives them a means to adapt to the world of action and to deal with it effectively.

Jung's only allusions to this fact are cryptically brief. As a result, almost all his followers except van der Hoop[1] seem to miss the principle involved. They assume that the *two* most developed processes are used in the favorite sphere (both extraverted or introverted) and that the other sphere is left to the mercy of the two inferior processes. . . .

Good type development thus demands that the auxiliary supplement the dominant process in two respects. It must supply a useful degree of balance not only between perception and judgment but *also between extraversion and introversion*. When it fails to do so it leaves the individual literally "unbalanced," retreating into the preferred world and consciously or unconsciously afraid of the other world. Such cases do occur and may seem to support the widespread assumption among Jungian analysts that the dominant and auxiliary are naturally both extraverted or both introverted; but such cases are not the norm: they are instances of insufficient use and development of the auxiliary.

It thus seems clear to me that those friends who consider me to be an extravert sense my extraverted intuition, whereas those who think I am an introvert are impressed by my introverted thinking. It follows that I use the first of my leading functions to communicate with some people, and I use the second of my leading functions with others. This recognition has led me to conclude that the types are a system of checks and balances. The functions alternate according to attitude, from most to least conscious or differentiated. Listing my functions according to degree of differentiation (downward, from most to least) and in terms of the attitude taken by each

---

1. This point has been appreciated in recent years by Wayne Detloff (1972, p. 70) and by Alex Quenk (1978).

function (whether extraverted or introverted), it is possible to give me a *type profile:*[2]

> extraverted intuition
> introverted thinking
> extraverted feeling
> introverted sensation.

From my type profile, a number of conclusions can be drawn. First, it should be noted that I have some of all four functions. However, I habitually take the extraverted attitude toward the tasks that call for the use of my intuition; I do not take the introverted ways of using intuition—I avoid, inhibit, or simply fail to recognize it. (Indeed, I have much trouble recognizing that introverted intuition is even valid; it frequently seems like a misuse of intuition.) Similarly, I have much trouble with the extraverted approach to thinking: It seems collective, unoriginal, and tiresome. The right way to think, for me, is introvertedly. When the task calls for feeling—as when a colleague asks me to a party—I think the extraverted approach is the only way to express feeling: I should go to the party because he or she wants me there. (Here I need a partner with introverted feeling to say "I don't want to go!", which defends one's own preferences and energy limitations. Such a response would help me see that I have a personal rather than an empathic or political stake in the matter.) Finally, I do have sensation, assiduously carried by my unconscious (and especially by my anima, which insists on its importance). This inferior, touchy sensation, however, is emphatically introverted, and terribly concerned with the comfort of my own body's interior at meals and at other times when visceral sensations, such as taste and hunger, predominate, and is usually indifferent to the extraverted side of sensation, such as the layout of a house or the route I take when going to a party.

My strong preference for a given attitude when using each of my functions makes me sensitive to the experience of some people and insensitive to the experience of others. For that reason, I tend to almost always be in harmony with some people and often in

---

2. I decided to use this term before I was aware of the "Typrofile," a trademark of the Typrofile Press that consists of a little face illustrating each of the 16 types identified by the Myers-Briggs Type Indicator. A reading of Schemel and Borbely's (1982) pamphlet will reveal the compatibility of my model with theirs, as well as the different emphasis of their approach.

trouble with others. Here is the profile of someone I manage almost never to offend:

> introverted sensation
> extraverted feeling
> introverted thinking
> extraverted intuition.

The person with this profile is my opposite, and one might think we are so different that we can hardly communicate with each other. In fact, this person is my oldest friend, and we have enjoyed talking to each other for 30 years, since we were prep school roommates. He became a businessman, I a doctor; he went to a Freudian analyst, I to a Jungian; he is a Republican, I a Democrat; he is, in his spare time, an athlete, I a scholar; and so on. We are compatible because we share the same attitude toward whatever topic we discuss, whether it involves feeling, sensation, thinking, or intuition. The fact that he is more advanced than I in terms of sensation and feeling makes him even more valuable to me; he completes my grasp of those areas. I think I do the same for him in other ways: my introverted thinking and my extraverted intuition buttress his.

A more important reason for our compatibility is our satisfaction with each other on the anima level. Our animas have each found someone with plenty of the dominant she considers important: His anima likes my intuition, since she has always wanted him to develop his extraverted intuition more; and my anima likes his sensation, since she likes me to be concerned with introverted sensation. If he had extraverted sensation, my anima would be irritated, not soothed, and I doubt he would like my intuition much if it were introverted.

The following is a profile of someone I more often offended— my companion in life for 13 years:

> introverted feeling
> extraverted sensation
> introverted intuition
> extraverted thinking.

A moment's comparison between my profile and his reveals that on any issue involving feeling, sensation, intuition, or thinking, his attitude—extraverted or introverted—will be the opposite of mine. This opposition has led to difficulties not only on the ego level (e.g., conflicts of will and genuine differences of opinion) but also on the anima level. The introverted sensation that my anima thinks most important is often ignored by his auxiliary in favor of extraverted sensation, and the orderly extraverted thinking that his anima prefers is lacking in my idiosyncratic introverted thinking.

My prep school roommate and I are alike in that we both have "irrational," or (as Myers would say) "perceiving," functions as our dominants, whereas my companion and I differ in that he has a "rational," or "judging," function as his dominant. He frequently has taken my perceptions for judgments, and I have taken his judgments for perceptions; we have often had to remind ourselves that my perceptions do not refute his judgments, and his judgments do not negate my perceptions.

Although I am instinctively more comfortable with my prep school roommate, I have learned more from my companion. My prep school roommate has tended to confirm the processes I use to arrive at my beliefs, if not the exact content of those beliefs. My companion has served to remind me continually that there is another process than the one I would normally use, and I suspect that I have done the same for him. Through him, I have learned about the introverted approach to intuition, the extraverted approach to sensation, the extraverted approach to thinking, and the introverted approach to feeling—all normally neglected when I function according to my instinctive profile. This learning has been difficult for me, but it has permitted me to progress in psychological understanding. I have begun to see that any problem of feeling, thinking, sensation, or intuition involves a choice between opposite extraverted *or* introverted approaches. I no longer believe that there is only one approach to a problem, and this awareness has extended my empathy for patients who may choose an option other than the one I propose as a result of my dominant attitude.

The model of psychological types I have been discussing in this paper retains the bipolar assumption that Singer and Loomis (1980) have recently challenged with new empirical testing. I have validated the bipolar assumption—this is, that thinking and feeling, and sensation and intuition, are poles of a single axis—by studying psychological types in interactions, in dreams, and through introspection and empathy. My model extends the bipolar assumption to its logical conclusion, namely, that not only the functions but their attitudes as well are opposites along a given axis. The strongest opposites are the axes themselves. The rational axis (whose poles are thinking and feeling) and the irrational axis (whose poles are intuition and sensation) are worlds apart, and the most significant single difference between individuals, it seems to me, occurs when the superior functions fall on different axes. Thus the perceiving types are all more alike, whether the dominant is extraverted or introverted, sensation or intuition; the judging types are all more alike, whether the dominant is introverted or extraverted, feeling or thinking; and the judging and perceiving types could not be more different.

Clinical Applications of the Model

Probably the most important influence on the kind of transference that an analysand will develop is the quality of the analyst's empathy as experienced by the analysand. (For an extraordinarily lucid discussion of the concept of empathy, see Basch 1983.) The relation of the analyst's type profile to that of the analysand can be predictive of the empathic understanding between analyst and analysand. Where the analyst's type profile matches the analysand's, the analyst's empathy is instinctive and easy. Where the analyst's type profile is not in harmony with the analysand's, there will be empathic failures. Easy empathy promotes an archetypal transference, as described by Edward Edinger (1973) in *Ego and Archetype*:

> Patients with a damaged ego-Self axis are most impressed in psychotherapy by the discovery that the therapist accepts them. Initially they cannot believe it. The fact of acceptance may be discredited by considering it only a professional technique having no genuine reality. However, if the acceptance of the therapist can be recognized as a fact, a powerful transference promptly appears. The source of this transference seems to be the projection of the Self, especially in its function as the organ of acceptance. At this point the central characteristics of the therapist-Self become prominent. The therapist as a person becomes the center of the patient's life and thoughts. The therapy sessions become the central points of the week. A center of meaning and order has appeared where previously there was chaos and despair. These phenomena indicate that a repair of the ego-Self axis is occurring. Meetings with the therapist will be experienced as a rejuvenating contact with life which conveys a sense of hope and optimism. (p. 40)

I think the obvious reason the analyst catches the projection of the Self in such a happy transference/countertransference is that his type profile corresponds to the lines of differentiation favored by the analysand's own Self. Such relationships are not unlike that between my prep school roommate and myself—long lasting and affirmative.

Past a certain point of Self-repair, however, they may be more comfortable than growth promoting.

When the analyst's type profile is markedly different from the analysand's, a stormy, quarrelsome transference/countertransference may result. Under such preconditions, both analyst and analysand may feel uneasy, as if they are about to quarrel, despite their best efforts to be responsive to each other. Yet such experiences of inner disagreement can lead to growth. In the analytic situation, when the analysand feels the analyst's empathy coming from an unexpected direction, the analysand is forced to consider the possibility of assuming an attitude (extraverted or introverted) other than the one he or she had instinctively chosen for the problem in thinking, feeling, sensation, or intuition that is being explored. Sometimes that possibility is unacceptable to him or her, and the experience of differing from the analyst strengthens the analysand's sense of who he or she is. As von Franz (1971, p. 52) has emphasized, one generally has the most difficulty with a person who has the same leading function as one's own but a different attitude. Sometimes, however, a complementary transference can develop on this basis.

Such a complementary therapeutic interaction took place between myself and an older analyst. Our profiles were as follows:

My profile	*Analyst's profile*
extraverted intuition	introverted intuition
introverted thinking	extraverted thinking
extraverted feeling	introverted feeling
introverted sensation	extraverted sensation

Because we were both irrational or perceiving types, we did not tend to judge or feel judged by each other's responses and thus could fully explore our differences of attitude. During this analysis, I enjoyed—and I believe my analyst shared this enjoyment—discovering ways to bend the dominant function in the other direction. Since our levels of differentiation within each function were relatively equal (allowing for differences of age and length of psychological development), no great feelings of envy or shame resulted when undeveloped areas were exposed. Despite our occasional competing viewpoints, our relationship was a challenging yet comfortable one. The attitudinal differences in our dominant and in our other functions were secondary to our shared value of perceiving, which formed our major approach to relationship. Had we both been rational, judging types, it is possible that a much more competitive, hostile interaction might have arisen, given a parallel list of functions, since we would have been more likely to judge each other while trying to create a relationship. However, I believe that a complementary relationship is also possible between individuals who have different attitudes but the same superior functions that lie on the rational axis.

On the other hand, only a slight difference in type profile may be the cause of strain within the analytic relationship. Below is my profile matched with that of a patient:

My profile	*Patient's profile*
extraverted intuition	introverted thinking
introverted thinking	extraverted sensation
extraverted feeling	introverted intuition
introverted sensation	extraverted feeling

To illustrate the strain that this slight difference produced, I want to quote from the case report, which was written for another purpose:

A young engineer who had excelled in school and at college, under pressure from a demanding father, was motivated by drug experiences and peers in the counterculture to drop out of his first job after college for the purpose of exploring "varieties of religious experience." He drifted to the West Coast and lived in various communal situations, where he experimented with his sexual as well as his religious feelings. He eventually tried to exchange his dominant heterosexual adaptation for a homosexual one, but he became a most absurd and unsuccessful homosexual, affecting a mincing, false feminine persona and a whorish attitude that were in comic contrast to his normally reserved and masculine presentation of self. He became silly and disorganized under the pressure of these experiments, and he was hospitalized for what appeared to be a psychosis. When he asked to see a "Jungian," he was referred from a day treatment center to an analyst.

After some exploration, the analyst concluded that the patient, in his attempt to undo his father's excessive demands, had turned his psyche inside out. He had fled to his inferior functions in an attempt to discover parts of himself that his father could not organize for him. Normally an introverted thinking type with reliable auxiliary extraverted sensation, he had turned first to his relatively inferior introverted intuition, which he explored through drugs and through participation in a religious cult. Then communal life had stimulated his inferior extraverted feeling, which was normally carried by his anima. He became anima-identified, enacting the part of an inferior extraverted feeling woman. To be sure, he was taking revenge on his father by enacting an unconscious caricature of the "feminine" role he had felt himself to have occupied in his original relation to his father. But the entire compensation, witty though it was, was ruining his life and psychotically distorting his personality. Sadly enough, he was really very like the compulsive engineer his father had wanted him to be.

The analyst took the tack of gently supporting the patient's return to adaptation through his superior functions and quietly discouraged the patient from further exploration of his inferior functions. He firmly refused the more floridly "Jungian" feeling-intuitive approach the patient had at first demanded. With this approach, the patient's near-hebephrenic silliness disappeared. He resumed heterosexual functioning, recovered his dominant introverted personality, and sought work in a less ambitious field related to engineering. (Sandner and Beebe 1982, pp. 315–16)

I read this case report aloud at a seminar on types that I gave at the Jung Institute in San Francisco in November 1982, and a person's response to the wording of my report helped me to see that my tone with regard to this patient was cool, almost at times dismissive. A partial explanation for the pejorative edge to some of my remarks is that there was a sociopathic side of the client (not discussed in the case report) that had forced a premature termination. Nevertheless I believe that my countertransference was based much more on my temperamental distaste for the introverted direction of my patient's intuition and the extraverted direction of his sensation. I was more appreciative of his introverted thinking and extraverted feeling. In other words, I was "in sync" with his rational axis and "out of sync" with his irrational axis. Whereas I helped him put his rational axis in order, I could only encourage him to leave his irrational axis alone.

In clinical work it is important to realize that typological problems are frequently expressed by complexes, as when an introverted feeling type is excessively self-critical in a too-heroic effort to set himself straight. To understand the inevitable relationship between types and complexes that produces normal and neurotic conflicts, one has to recognize that characteristic archetypal personages carry the various functions according to their degree of differentiation within a given individual's type profile. Jung frequently pointed out that the anima carries the inferior function in a man and that the animus carries this function in a woman. I believe that the other functions, even if relatively differentiated from the unconscious, also carry hints of their archetypal origin: They too can be assigned to mythological figures. I have found that in the dreams of men, the superior function is frequently symbolized by a hero figure, who is the ego-ideal for the correct use of this function. The auxiliary function is frequently symbolized by a father, or *senex*, figure, and the third function by a son, or *puer*, figure. (In women, the analogous figures would be the heroine, the mother, and the daughter, or *puella*; the fourth function would be carried by an animus figure.)

A recognition of which figures carry the respective functions makes the dynamics of my analytic relationship with the patient in the case report more comprehensible. The following are our type profiles, with the archetypal figures identified.

My profile	*Patient's profile*
extraverted intuition (hero)	introverted thinking (hero)
introverted thinking (father)	extraverted sensation (father)
extraverted feeling (son)	introverted intuition (son)
introverted sensation (anima)	extraverted feeling (anima)

The object relations in the typological interaction that characterized my relationship with this patient can now be made explicit. It was through the use of my auxiliary introverted thinking that I could function as a father to his hero: I could authoritatively support the return of his introverted thinking to its rightful position of dominance within his psyche. At the same time, however, my own heroic extraverted intuition tended to overpower his weaker introverted intuition; he could only have felt belittled and dominated, and perhaps he was inspired to seek revenge in sociopathy. Equally, my anima, with her demanding introverted sensation, may have undermined many of his efforts to mount a strong fatherly auxiliary of extraverted sensation, and it was actually in this area that his sociopathy made its appearance. I could, on the other hand, bring a spontaneous *puer* appreciation to the comically tricksterish aspects of his anima, since my *puer* and his anima both carried extraverted feeling. I believe that my ability to respond to him on this level touched a healthy core within his ostensibly hebephrenic silliness and helped him adopt a more appropriate style of humor.

The recognition of the archetypal figures as expressive of the hierarchy of functions within the type profile enables one to make type diagnoses from dreams. In dreams in which a father and son or a mother and daughter appear together, the typological characteristics of these inner figures determine the nature of the second (auxiliary) and third functions. If the bipolar assumption is used, the presence of a clearly extraverted-feeling mother implies an introverted-thinking daughter. Other dreams in which *puella* figures appear can be used to determine whether the third function is indeed introverted thinking. Once the contrasexual figure carrying the inferior function appears, it is usually possible to complete the type profile. (One may have to reject several hypotheses before one finally gets a profile that satisfies the data.) It is on this basis that I have delineated with precision my type profile and those of my friends and patients.

In my own case, I had a series of dreams in which a thinking-type father was interacting with a feeling-type son. Later, a Chinese laundress whose activities were clearly suggestive of introverted sensation made her appearance, and this anima figure confirmed for me that introverted sensation was my inferior function. (Testing done with the Myers-Briggs Type Indicator early in the course of my analysis supported the findings from my dreams.)

Jung's "color-code" can also be used to make precise diagnoses of psychological types from dreams (see Jung 1959, par. 588). Jung correlates green (occasionally brown) with sensation, yellow with intuition, red with feeling, and blue with thinking. When one of the archetypal figures in a dream is dressed in or otherwise associated with one of these colors, the function carried by that figure may be established. Some of the *puer* figures in my dreams have had red hair or have worn red; knowing that the *puer* is associated with the third function and that red is suggestive of feeling has helped me confirm that feeling is my third function. I have had to scrutinize carefully the figures in my dreams as well as the operation of my feeling function in real life to become convinced that my feeling is typically extraverted. (Knowing that feeling is something of a *puer* has helped me understand that I will sometimes disappoint people by apparently being present with my extraverted feeling and then suddenly unavailable. This is an area in which I need to do further work.)

By observing over a long period of time one's own dreams and those of one's patients, it is possible to establish the exact profiles that are needed to explicate the therapeutic interaction in typological terms.

Summary

A model of psychological types and some clinical applications of the model have been offered as a way of using Jung's theory of psychological types more precisely and dynamically. Basic to the model are two assumptions. The first, which owes much to the pioneering work of Katharine Briggs and Isabel Myers, is that a person develops a profile based on preferential use of four of the possible eight types that represent the complete (extraverted and introverted) range of the four functions. The other four types in any individual are truly in shadow, and if they develop at all, it is only in response to the challenges of intimate relationships. This incompleteness of normal type development is the result of a system of checks and balances at one's disposal in the extraverted and introverted deployment of the various functions.

The second assumption, drawn from observation of the way functions are personified in dreams, is that psychological types, although functions of consciousness, differentiate according to an *a priori* archetypal plan out of an unconscious matrix. I believe that the four functions are ordered according to a scheme that has a hero/heroine figure (imaging the superior function) compensated by an anima/animus figure (carrying the inferior function) and assisted by a father/mother (holding the auxiliary function) and son/daughter (expressing the third function). This archetypal order is enormously helpful in identifying and validating an individual's type profile from his dreams, and it has profound implications for that individual's behavior in typological interactions with others.

One's type profile inevitably affects one's interactions with other persons who may have similar, somewhat different, or very different type profiles. Such interactions among types play a significant role in the dynamics of any intimate relationship, including the therapeutic relationship, where they form one of the complications of transference and countertransference.

References

Basch, M. F. 1983. Empathic understanding: A review of the concept and some theoretical considerations. *Journal of the American Psychoanalytic Association* 31/1:101–26.

Briggs, K. C., and Myers, I. B. 1979. *Manual: The Myers-Briggs type indicator.* Palo Alto, Calif.: Consulting Psychologists Press.

Detloff, W. 1972. Psychological types: Fifty years after. *Psychological Perspectives* 3/1:62–73.

Edinger, E. F. 1973. *Ego and archetype.* New York: Penguin Books.

Franz, M. L. von. 1971. The inferior function. In *Jung's typology*, pp. 1–54. New York: Spring Publications.

Jung, C. G., 1923. *Psychological types.* New York: Harcourt Brace.

————. 1959. A study in the process of individuation. In *Collected works,* 9/1:290–354. Princeton: Princeton University Press.

————. 1971. *Psychological types.* In *Collected works,* vol. 6. Princeton: Princeton University Press.

Myers, I. B., and Myers, P. B. 1980. *Gifts differing.* Palo Alto, Calif.: Consulting Psychologists Press.

Plaut, A. 1972. Analytical psychologists and psychological types: Comment on replies to a survey. *Journal of Analytical Psychology* 17/2:143–47.

Quenk, A. 1978. Psychological types: The auxiliary function and the analytical process. Unpublished thesis for the Inter-Regional Society of Jungian Analysts.

Sandner, D., and Beebe, J. 1982. Psychopathology and analysis. In *Jungian analysis,* M. Stein, ed., pp. 294–334. La Salle, Ill., and London: Open Court.

Schemel, G. J., and Borbely, J. A. 1982. *Facing your type.* Wernersville, Penn.: Typrofile Press.

Singer, J., and Loomis, M. 1980. Presenting the Singer-Loomis inventory of personality. In *Money, food, drink, and fashion and analytic training.* Proceedings of the Eighth International Congress for Analytical Psychology, J. Beebe, ed., pp. 386–97. Fellbach-Oeffingen, West Germany: Bonz, 1983.

Transference/ Countertransference Between Woman Analyst and the Wounded Girl Child

Betty De Shong Meador

For a woman to grow into her fullness, she must find her way to the feminine aspects of the Self. Her ego will then reflect, express, and root in the divine feminine. That is to say, aspects of that complex energy we call the archetypal feminine will inform her ego orientation.

A woman who carries an ill-formed ego due to difficulties in early childhood has particular problems relating to the archetypal feminine. The wound the child sustains from inadequate parenting lives into her adulthood in the form of low self-esteem and an unstable relationship to womanliness and to herself as a woman. This woman's self-worth is further undermined by real and perceived imbalances in the culture in favor of men and the masculine. To the extent that the wounded girl child adapts herself to the culturally more favored male attitudes and values in order to enhance her self-esteem, she blinds her ego to her natural feminine

Betty De Shong Meador, Ph.D., is a Jungian analyst in private practice in the San Diego area. A member of the San Diego and the Los Angeles Societies of Jungian Analysts, she received B.A. and M.A. degrees from the University of Texas and a Ph.D. from United States International University in San Diego. She has authored numerous articles on client-centered therapy and on the feminine in Jungian psychology and is currently at work on translations of the poetry of the Sumerian goddess, Inanna.

ground. This woman enters adulthood with a weak ego, dominated by collectively held attitudes to which she clings for survival. Within her psyche she carries a wounded child thwarted in her natural development. Nevertheless, this child carries the seeds of female instinctuality that can lead the woman to the Self.

Much has been written concerning the treatment of the wounded child within the adult in a therapy setting. In this paper I look at one aspect of the transference/countertransference between woman client and woman analyst as that wounded child appears in the analysis and begins to push for integration.

On a larger scale, I am looking at a passage or a crossing over, as a woman shifts the support of her female self from the patriarchy to the archetypal feminine. In this process she will let go of attitudes she has imposed on herself from the outer culture and foster those attitudes spawned by her instinct, as these begin to appear to her in dreams, imagination, and feeling.

On an archetypal scale, this crossing is the task of the shifting age as we move from Pisces to Aquarius. The goddess in her many forms is reemerging into a conscious place in the pantheon. This enormous archetypal event is manifesting itself in myriad ways in our world, not the least of which is its appearance in the unsuspecting, unprepared psyches of analyst and analysand.

Ironically, the very woundedness of the girl child within carries a knowledge of the divine feminine. The wound, while it is seriously incapacitating and emotionally painful, implies a secret loyalty to feminine instinctuality. The wound implicitly says, *this is not right.* It is not right that femaleness be constrained or despised. Woman's secret, sometimes her shame, is that she is linked by blood to the banished Whore of Babylon as well as to Mary the Mother of God. The woman *intimately* feels instinctual aspects of the feminine that have been repressed and denied by the culture. The archetypal patriarchal backdrop to our culture manifests itself with a stubborn conservatism. As the new archetypal mode—the goddess—emerges, it necessarily appears first in the psyches of individuals who must suffer the weight of it within an alien or hostile culture. The old cultural forms, like a bad marriage or neurotic defenses, tend to live on past their usefulness.

The particular problem for women who are trying to foster and nourish a wounded girl child is that this child must ultimately be grounded in the feminine instinctual aspects of the Self. Feminine instinctuality in the culture lives in some unsavory places. The witch has carried it with her intuitive wisdom and psychic healing. Outrageous women have carried it as they fling their proud sexuality in the face of the proper fathers. Certain collective manifestations of the feminine have been split off and ostracized from viable cultural expression just as they are split off in individual psyches. Little wonder, then, that women tremble when the goddess appears with her promise to heal the wounded child.

I want to look at the blossoming of the seeds of love of the feminine that the wounded child carries. I want to explore a particular transference/countertransference manifestation and some of its implications. I would like to present this situation in the form of a fairy tale. The tale is told from the analyst's point of view, but it could as easily be told from the point of view of any woman.

This is a fairy tale about two women working together in a close, intimate relationship. It begins with one woman coming to the other for help on certain problems in her life. The woman who is helper has learned a lot from books, from elders, from going for help herself, and has had years of experience listening to women who come to her. She thinks she can handle what might emerge in this intimate relationship. If she gets baffled, she knows several people to whom she could turn for advice.

One day, to the helper woman's great surprise, bewilderment, even shame and embarrassment, a powerful immediate intense erotic emotion wells up in her toward the woman who has come for help. Her face reddens; she dares not speak of it.

A confused whirling of images follows. She remembers learning, indeed believing, the wrongful destructivenss of seducing anyone who comes to her for help. She had felt safe. *Men* had talked a lot about the problems of erotic feelings toward women they helped, and perhaps someday she might love in a lustful way some handsome man who came to her. But never in her wildest dream did she imagine Eros would direct her gaze toward a woman.

Her feelings were out of control. Luckily, an elder to whom she talked was designated a control analyst. Surely she would know what to do. The two of them talked for a long time. They talked for weeks. "How could this happen?" asked the bewildered helper. "I do love women. I feel such compassion for women. My heart goes out to the woundedness they bring. Yet you know as well as I how strongly directed toward men my erotic feelings have been."

The control analyst suggested many possible unravelings of this tangled problem. As it was the custom in this tribe for the initiates to show their readiness by presenting in written form the story of one particular person they had helped, the control analyst suggested that the poor helper write the story of this most difficult relationship. And she did.

The helper, still not really understanding what had happened, went before the elders appointed to perform this final initiation. They all happened to be men, and they too were baffled, offering many new reasons why such a thing might occur. The helper survived the initiation and became a full-fledged, if somewhat confused, member of the tribe.

The helper settled into her new role. She had a wonderfully rich relationship with the man in her life. Perhaps the feelings she had had toward this woman were "a stage in her development" as the elders had taught her to say. Perhaps she was now in a new phase of her growth, and though she still did not understand what had happened, perhaps the memories of it would fade away.

They did not. Even worse. New women came to her for help. More and more often the burst of erotic feelings arose as these women told their stories. No longer could she console herself that the first experience was a one-time, atypical but necessary, event having to do with a stage in her development. Now her eroticism poured indiscriminately. She never knew toward whom it might flow. She felt in utter despair. "Oh God," she prayed, "must I leave the man I love? What does this mean? Would you have me torn in two?"

As if in answer to her prayer, a great goddess came to her in a dream. She spoke with clarity. "The patriarchy is finished," she said. "Can you not see that? Do you not see the death of it in the two graves you and the other women are preparing? Do you not see the great reed pillar I have implanted on the graves? The reed pillar is my image, my epiphany. Wherever it stands, I am there in all my power. It is my power which stands on the grave of the patriarchy. You must hasten to gather more reeds. Go with the other women. Build the pillars in my image."

The great goddess told her many other things in the dream. "I come to you," she said, "in a very strong form, the erotic. You have forgotten how to love me. I will come to you again and again until you learn. I am teaching you to love me, to love womanliness, to love woman, to love your womanly self. I use strong medicine."

The woman awoke in awe. She felt relieved, felt the revelation was an opening, a beginning, an entrance into a mystery. She began in every way she knew how to worship the great goddess. Slowly, the difficult erotic feelings she had had toward women she helped began to subside. Strangely enough, another phenomenon seemed to appear with their fading. Woman after woman of those who came to her told the following story: "I have always been strongly heterosexual, but the strangest thing is happening . . . ," or, "I have been married 25 years, happily, and, suddenly, for no reason, these feeings have arisen . . . ," and always the end of the story was one of a great erotic arousal, as consuming and overwhelming as it was surprising that it was directed toward women.

The helper bowed in her heart in reverence to the great goddess when she heard these stories, and she blessed the day the goddess had come to her in a dream. She felt the great goddess had focused her sight and clarified difficulties she had suffered all her life.

This tale stands on its own as an example of the healing the goddess can bring and also an example of the hazards passion carries when the feminine erupts in the psyche. The goddess comes in many forms to women. While she offers solid instinctual ground for the wounded child, she carries as well the dangerous allure of any archetype, a temptation for the ego to enfold itself in her power.

As a part of my own attempt to relate to this archetype, I have begun to study the goddess Inanna, the most powerful of the Sumerian goddesses, and a precursor to Ishtar and Astarte. Synchronistically, I was unaware that Sylvia Perera had also been affected by this goddess. The appearance of Perera's (1981) book, *Descent to the Goddess*, and the recent publication by Wolkstein and Kramer (1983) of a new translation of poetry about Inanna suggest that Inanna has something to say to us at this moment.

The poetry about Inanna was written about 2500 B.C., and her stature as a Mesopotamian goddess probably predates the writing by at least a thousand years. She carries religious expression of the divine feminine prior to the beginning of the patriarchy and the submission of the goddess to the monotheistic masculine. That is to say, she carries aspects of the feminine that were repressed by the patriarchy but that women continue to know in their deepest instinctual selves. These hidden aspects, then, are part of the feminine ground the wounded child seeks in her effort to be fully woman.

In the myth of Inanna's descent to the Underworld, which Perera so ably explores, we learn that Inanna goes to the Underworld by her own choice. The first line of the text says, "SHE in great heaven set her ear to great earth." Line four says, "MY LADY left heaven, abandoned earth, went down below." The word for *ear* in Sumerian also means wisdom or mind. For Inanna to set her ear to the earth and to the Underworld is for her to attend to it with her wisdom.

Inanna goes to the Underworld to meet her older sister, Erishkegal, who reigns there. Here, then, is a pattern of the feminine. The upper world goddess, Inanna, the highly cultivated, civilized one, seeks the initiation of the deep and dark primal chthonic powers her older sister holds in the underworld. There Inanna endures a divesting of her power, death, decay, and resurrection.

Another group of poems about Inanna are from the Sacred Marriage Ritual, a New Year's rite. In these poems we find not only the young goddess in all the flutter of courtship and first love but also the bold goddess exalting her body as it longs for sexual fulfillment, and the wise and benevolent goddess who pours her bounty from the "diamond starred" storehouse, the "radiant storehouse of fate." Here are my translations of three poems in which the goddess exalts her body.

Vulva Song

I, the Lady
in the house of holy lapis
in sanctuary I pray
I say a holy prayer

I am the Queen of Heaven
let chanters recite this chant
let singers sing this song
let my bridegroom rejoice with me
let wild bull Dumuzi rejoice

let the words fall out of their mouths
let them sing in the time of their youth
let the song rise up in Nippur
a gift for the son divine

I the Lady sing to praise him
let chanters recite this chant
I Inanna sing to praise him
I give him my vulva song

peg my vulva
my star sketched horn of the Dipper
moor my slender boat of heaven
my new moon crescent cunt beauty

I wait an unplowed desert
fallow field for the wild ducks
my high mound longs for the floodlands

my vulva hill is open
this maid asks who will plow it
vulva moist in the floodlands
the queen asks who brings the ox

the king, Lady, will plow it
Dumuzi, king, will plow it

plow then man of my heart
holy water-bathed loins

holy Ninegal[1] am I

Holy Song

this song is holy

let me tell you where I'm coming from
my vulva is
the power place
a royal sign

---

1. Another name for Inanna.

I rule with cunt power
I see with cunt eyes
this is where
I'm coming from

An[2]
fit me out
with my vulva
I live right here
in this soft slit
I live right here
my field wants hoeing
this is my holy word
a dazzling palace
without its sun
I want you Dumuzi
your bough raised to my cunt
Dumuzi
you belong in this house
I looked at everyone
Dumuzi I call you
it's you I want
for prince

Dumuzi, beloved of Enlil[3]
even my mother and father adore you

listen
I will scrub my skin with soap
I will rinse all over with water
I will dry myself with linen
I will lay out mighty love clothes
        I know how exactly
I will look so fine
I will make you feel like a king

Poem in Woman's Tongue[4]

the Good City temple
Eridu temple
is fixed up right

---

2. God of heaven.
3. God of air.
4. This poem was written in eme-sal, a dialect of Sumerian used for the speech of goddesses and their servants.

the Moon God temple
temple of Sin
shines radiant

An's temple
Eanna
is armed to protect the day

cloud-like Ezida
head of temples
overflows with blessings for you

GOOD IS THE NAME WE GIVE THIS DAY
DAY OF THE LAPIS BED

holy fire god
holy Gibil
purifies the great sacred room
sanctifies it fit for a queen
fills the reed house
cleans the storehouse
pours the sacred water blessing

he wakes the sleeping day
by shouting its name

LOOK
THE DAY OF THE BED

the Day the lord exalts the woman
the Day she gives life to her lord
she gives harvest power to her lord
gives the harvest scepter to her lord

SHE WANTS IT
she wants the bed
she wants it

the joy of her heart bed
she wants the bed
she wants it

the sweet thigh bed
she wants the bed
she wants it

the king's bed
she wants the bed
she wants it

the queen's bed
she wants the bed
she wants it

with his sweet thing
with his sweet thing bed
with his sweet thing

the joy of her heart bed
with his sweet thing bed
with his sweet thing

the sweet thigh bed
with his sweet thing bed
with his sweet thing

the king's bed
with his sweet thing bed
with his sweet thing

the queen's bed
with his sweet thing bed
with his sweet thing

she makes the bed for him
she lays out the bed

she makes the bed for him
she lays out the bed

I want to repeat that these poems are about only one aspect of this goddess, the goddess singing praises to her body. After the consummation of the marriage, Inanna becomes the gift giver, the weaver of fate, watching over the "house of life." The final words of one of these poems, in which Inanna pours bounty from the storehouse, are "it is strong! it is strong!" Her bounteous gifts nourish, enliven, and strengthen. She is the epitome of fully realized womanhood, strong in itself.

As a way of understanding more deeply the complexity of this goddess, a group of us worked with these poems over a period of months, finally developing a performance of them, which we have presented a few times. The work with the poems has meant many things to us, not the least of which was the delight, the good fun, of women enjoying ribaldry. What came to be the underlying experience of the performance, however, was experience of the sacred. We put on the robes and roles of priestesses to the goddess and moved through the poems in that basic attitude.

A whole variety of reactions have surfaced from those of us who took part in the performance as well as from people in the audiences who viewed it. The one reaction that comes repeatedly and that pertains to this paper is the conflict between the old gods and the new. Dreams have come that say, on the one hand, that Jehovah unequivocally disapproves of Inanna and what she evokes in women. Other women have dreamed, following our performance, of great violence being done to them by men. All of us have struggled with a sense of shame that we dared to sing exaltation to our bodies in a public place.

On the other hand, powerful eruptions of change have appeared in dreams connected with the performance of the Inanna poems. More than once these dreams contained an image of a nuclear blast along with images of the woman dreamer leaving behind her former relationship to the collective fathers. I take these dreams to be introducing an image of the new age, the fission which releases a new kind of energy altogether.

For women to leave behind their former daughterly relationship to the patriarchy and ground themselves in their own feminine nature is a shift in loyalty of huge proportion. It reverberates on the personal level, as this woman writes: "It connects me with a small piece of earth on which to plant my soul," while in the past "this flame would leap out briefly, tempt fate, and disappear quickly in shame and fear."

The shift also reverberates archetypally. The reemergence of the goddess, the archetypal feminine, shakes the archetypal status quo. A new face of God appears, and She is a woman. Not without great upheaval will She take her place beside the gods who have enjoyed dominance for 3000 years.

For certain women, in addition to a cognitive awareness of her appearance, the goddess archetype is an active force in the psyche, coming to them in dreams, fantasies, visions, and feelings. This energy is life changing. It will lead women to carve out new forms for their lives, new channels of expression out in the world of the twentieth and twenty-first centuries. From the energy of the goddess informing their lives, women will discover forms which have no precedents, and these individually carved forms will be the expression of each woman's individual perception. This carving of new forms requires great courage and a devotion to one's individual vision. It requires that one's feet be planted solidly on feminine ground.

Jung has in his own life, in his writings, and in his work with patients exposed the enormous power of archetypal energies in forming and shaping the direction of an individual life. When a great shift is occurring in that drama, as it is now, the shift, as Jung (1959) described it in his book, *Aion*, necessarily produces conflict, not only between people with differing loyalties but also between the voices carried inside oneself. It cannot be otherwise. Perhaps for generations this conflict will continue to manifest itself. I believe we now have the opportunity and the obligation of carrying the conflict with more consciousness of its relationship to the new age, that is, to the struggle of the goddess to achieve Her place in the godhead.

References

Jung, C. G. 1959. *Aion: Researches into the phenomenology of the self.* In *Collected works,*, vol. 9, part 2. Princeton: Princeton University Press.
Perera, S. 1981. *Descent to the goddess.* Toronto: Inner City Books.
Wolkstein, D., and Kramer, S. N. 1983. *Inanna.* New York: Harper & Row.

Mother, Father, Teacher, Sister: Transference/Countertransference Issues with Women in the First Stage of Animus Development

Florence L. Wiedemann

In this paper, I hope to clarify the analyst's and the analysand's part in the interactional fields set up around certain developmental issues. These interactional fields of transference/countertransference are very much like those experienced in other human relationships, except that in the therapeutic relationship the focus is entirely on analysands, on attempting to understand them and to help them change. Here I will discuss mainly mothering and fathering attitudes that I have experienced in working with young women who find themselves in the first stage of animus development.

After observing women's dreams that revolve around issues of authority and competency and around relationship to men, a pattern formed in my mind. Concurrently Polly Eisendrath-Young was observing and describing similar images and stages of animus devel-

Florence L. Wiedemann, Ph.D., is president of the Analytical Psychology Association of Dallas, secretary of the Inter-Regional Society of Jungian Analysts, and is in private practice in Dallas, Texas. A graduate in clinical psychology of the University of Texas Health Science Center at Dallas and a Diplomate Jungian Analyst from the Inter-Regional Society of Jungian Analysts, she is an adjunct professor at Southern Methodist University and is co-author of a book in progress entitled *Female Authority*.

opment. We are now writing a book (Eisendrath-Young and Wiedemann 1984) in which we discuss these issues. This present paper
represents part of that larger endeavor.

First, a definition. By animus I mean the tendency in women
that directs attention toward actuality; an enterprising spirit of courage, determination, vigor that moves ahead with authority and force-
fulness. These qualities of animus allow a woman to be effective,
powerful, and competent in the world. In addition, animus signifies
a woman's feeling relationship to a man, to men in general, to
patriarchal culture, and to spiritual life. For women, the functioning
of the animus occurs intrapersonally and intrapsychically, and in
relation to the wider culture.

The classical Jungian sense of animus development assumes
"normal" ego development and identity development in the first
half of life, followed by a crisis that leads to second-half-of-life
development. The animus, as a second-half development, is seen as
the function that bridges ego-consciousness and the unconscious,
connecting a woman to the reality of her spiritual and deeper
psychological life.

In intrapsychic terms, the animus can be regarded as a complex
with an archetypal core that takes form as the self–other differentiation occurs in the first three years of life. As a girl grows, her ego
development and animus development ideally go hand in hand:
Feminine identity and animus development go forward together.
The more the contrasexual animus element is repressed, the more
the girl is cut off from her own sense of authority and the more she
sees the masculine as "the alien and dangerous other."

The stages of animus development, as derived from clinical
observation, correspond to mythological themes; each stage, moreover, is associated with a particular developmental arrest or pathology. The first stage, which will be described in this paper, is named
"Animus as Outsider." In this stage, a woman's relationship to her
unconscious masculine potential is so undeveloped that the world
of masculine figures and authority is filled with threatening possibilities. To this she responds with mistrust and fear. Mythologically,
this stage is reflected in the theme of the rape of Persephone, the
young daughter of Demeter who was taken by Hades, god of the
underworld and brother of Zeus.

The succeeding images of animus development, which will not
be discussed in this paper but will be developed in the book co-
authored with Polly Eisendrath-Young, are "Animus as Father, God,

Patriarch"; "Animus as Youth, Hero and Lover"; "Animus as the Partner Within"; and "Animus as Androgyne." Each stage is represented by a mythological theme, which depicts the experience and integration of animus within it and indicates its archetypal-developmental underpinnings.

For the final stages, women today are forming a new archetypal image. Since human nature has evolved since prehistoric times, there is no reason to think we have reached the endpoint of conscious development. Recent discoveries in biology and quantum physics suggest that an expanding collective consciousness exerts a reciprocal influence on the collective unconscious. New ways women are finding to be in relationship to themselves, to one another, to their children, to men, and to the larger culture are being forged by hundreds of thousands of contemporary persons. These women are forming the pattern of "Animus as Androgyne."

In the first phase, though, a woman has a troubled relationship to the masculine, both within herself and in the world. In dreams, men are typically imaged as rapists, killers, members of motorcycle gangs, or frightening, pursuing figures. In the wider social and professional worlds, her sense of competency, self-discipline, assertiveness, and effective instrumentality is lacking. In relationships with actual men, she feels overwhelmed, invaded, and abused, and in reality she often is abused, ignored, or dominated. A number of marital disturbances are related to this phase, since the "masculine" within and without is not trusted.

Neumann (1959) named this earliest phase of a woman's consciousness "self-conservation." In the self-conserving phase, it is characteristic for women to remain psychologically, and often sociologically, in a female group, such as a mother clan, and to maintain primary relationships with mother groups ("above") and with the daughter groups ("below"). This attachment to the feminine bond coincides with splitting away from the masculine and with a feeling of alienation toward it (Neumann 1959, p. 63). Typical problems of this phase have to do with the woman feeling herself to be weak, "witchy," or monstrous.

Women imprisoned in concentration camps, possessed by demon lovers, chased by rapists and burglars—these are the typical dream motifs. The demon in possession of her hates God and life. This woman may feel she lives in a world where she has no rights and does not belong. She feels devalued and outcast; she lacks confidence; she sees herself as fat, dumb, inarticulate; she cannot live an authentic life. The negative masculine is bent upon criticizing her. His voice tells her she is old, unloved, uncreative, useless, which prevents her from feeling confident in her own authentic goodness.

The woman who feels men to be "alien outsiders" constellates predictable transference and countertransference reactions and attitudes in treatment by a woman therapist. These are the typical attitudes of mother, father, teacher, and sister.

Such an analysand is still encased in a symbiotic mother–daughter relationship, with the result that she has a poor sense of separate, individual identity. This lack of separation from the mother complex, added to the strength of the negative masculine complex, paralyzes the woman. Ulanov (1979) comments: "Something in the daughter was not fed, was not held, was not seen by her mother, father, school, boys and others" (p. 21). Part of the analyst's Demeter mother role, then, is to feed back clinical intuition of who the "baby daughter" is. Empathic, reflective listening and dream watching form the early basis of holding, feeding, mirroring, accepting, and reflecting her identity back to her. Establishment of emotional rapport makes space for the fledgling ego to grow, and later this same bond becomes the effective basis of requiring action and change from her. In addition, I feed back the results of clinical tests: the Strong-Campbell Interest Inventory (Strong and Campbell 1976), which shows her interests; the Myers-Briggs Type Indicator (Briggs and Myers 1979), with explanation of her psychological type and readings from *Gifts Differing* (Myers and Myers 1980) and *Please Understand Me* (Kersey and Bates 1978); the results of the Minnesota Multiphasic Personality Inventory (MMPI; Hathaway and McKinley 1966).

Having been rejected or overprotected, or both, these analysands make a terrific demand for emotional nourishment. They present themselves as requiring a great deal of affection, mirroring, attention, "holding," and encouragement. They also show a handicap in the abililty to take in and to digest the nourishment that is given. They seem infinitely hungry, and analysis can turn into endless feedings without any change taking place, particularly if the analyst identifies with the archetypal mother. The analysand's anxiety about identity can paralyze the therapist.

This anxiety breeds docility, clinging, helplessness, and a poignant search for support, nurturance, and reassurance. This woman feels inferior and avoids taking initiative or showing self-determination. Except for desiring belonging and acceptance, she refrains from making demands on others.

These women submerge their individuality, subordinate their tastes and desires, deny whatever vestiges of identity they may possess apart from others, and often submit to abuse and intimidation, all in the hope of avoiding isolation. Sometimes they have little choice. Financially dependent, burdened by child care, lacking education and skills, they feel paralyzed and empty if left to their own devices. They search for guidance in fulfilling the simplest tasks and in making routine decisions.

Passive-dependent individuals such as these often seek a single, all-powerful "magic helper," a partner in whom they can place their trust, depend on to supply the few comforts they want, and protect them from having to assume responsibilities or face the competitive struggles of life. Supplied with a nurturant and dependable partner, they may function quite well, be sociable, and display affection and generosity to others. Deprived of these supports, however, they withdraw and become tense, despondent, and forlorn. Men who choose to relate to them are equally dependent, but often they are seen as abusive of their wives.

The absence of self-confidence is apparent in these women's postures, voices and mannerisms. They tend to be overly cooperative and prefer to yield and placate rather than to assert. Large groups and noisy "affairs" are abhorrent to them. They go to great pains to avoid public attention by underplaying their attractiveness and achievements.

Friends often view these women as generous and thoughtful, but they may note an apologetic and obsequious tone in their voices. Neighbors and colleagues are impressed by their humility, their cordiality and graciousness, and by the "softness" and gentility of their behavior.

Beneath the surface of this affability, however, there lies a plaintive and solemn visage, searching for assurances of acceptance and approval. These features are more clearly manifest under conditions of stress. At those times, there are more overt signs of helplessness and of a clinging attitude; there may be actual pleading for encouragement.

Although these features of low-level animus development can be seen in many psychological types, their most frequent occurrence seems to coincide with the introverted, intuitive, feeling, perceptive type (INFP). Each type is vulnerable to some sort of pathology. This type of woman's strength is predominantly affiliative, but she has poor instrumental skills in relating to the world. Not rooted in facts, unable to produce or to make judgments and decisions with self-confidence, these women, unlike more "androgynous" women who apparently are capable of using both decision-making and affiliative processes and who can move in and out of thinking and feeling as required by the situation, seem out of their element in situations that require higher level animus and ego-functioning (Padgett et al. 1982).

Because such an INFP woman is still engulfed in "the mother," she has difficulty in separating her own identity from her mother's. A relationship to the maternal, accepting aspects of the analyst can free such a woman from her own mother enough to redefine some of these qualities for herself. The period of loving, accepting, and mirroring "the girl" can last several years.

The majority of my women patients who are of this type are under 35 years of age. On the MMPI scale 2, the Depression scale, and scale 0, the Introversion-Isolation scale, are very elevated, more than two standard deviations above normal. This suggests that these persons are overly sensitive to criticism, that they tend to be lonely and have poor interpersonal relations, and that they feel helpless and unable to change. They have a strong need for affection, which is reflected in an elevated scale 3 on the MMPI. At worst, their depression and isolation lead to withdrawal and schizoidlike characteristics. Often conversion symptomatology is part of this, the body showing lassitude and malaise; also *globus hystericus*, anorexia, and other psychosomatic symptoms are not uncommon. These problems of the body reflect the relationship to the mother complex, on which Marion Woodman (1980, 1982) has done work. The MMPI scale 4, which reflects aggression, anger, rebellion, determination, discipline (i.e., "yang qualities") is frequently diminished, suggesting an inability to express aggression. Aggression can be expressed only in passive-aggressive ways. These tactics are self-defeating and make her personal relationships worse while increasing her feelings of personal inferiority and loneliness.

Young women of this kind exhibit a negative mother complex. They have either never had realistic or positive enough mothering and are therefore searching for an ideal situation, or they have had an engulfing mother who never released her daughter to live her own life. Such young women often say their mother was their best friend. They insist that she was ideal and perfect and that they had a wonderful relationship. Often they come into therapy when the mother has died. Then the symbiosis is broken and the girl is psychically bleeding to death.

The following is a dream early in the analysis of a young woman who fits the description I have outlined:

Dream: *I was picking Tom up at the airport. My father and my brother were also there. My father's brother was driving all of us home in the car. He drove into a ditch. I was badly scratched, and I cried: "Check and see if Billy [who is 14] and Christy [8] are all right." We pulled them out, but they weren't people. They were long cocoonlike things. There were three of them. The darker one was Billy, the lighter one was Christy. We opened Billy and Christy, and they weren't human. They were big worms, like larvae. In Christy's larva, she was cut and bleeding, and I was trying to decide if she was alive. I didn't open the third cocoon, but it looked smaller, like a baby larva. I was looking at the cut. Is she dead? She was alive, but I didn't know how badly hurt, or if she was going to make it.*

In association to the wounded Christy-larva, the analysand said that she wanted to get rid of the hurt inside. The dream suggests to me a developmental lag at three stages: the baby, the young girl, and the young animus. These we would have to let form and heal.

The mother this young woman experienced "loved too much," contained too long, held her and ensnared her, and left her with "Garden of Eden" ideas about the world. These resulted in disenchantment with reality. Other analysands, however, have experienced rejecting mothers who never really looked on the infant faces with joy and never reflected back their value and worth. To counterbalance this, the analyst must be the mother who finds the value in the analysand and connects her to the Self. As she develops, the analyst must release her and allow and encourage her to leave, freeing her from the mother–daughter relationship so that she can become a woman and a mother herself.

As long as the positive transference continues, in which the daughter loves the mother, everything goes well. In reflecting the Self to her, I not only feel empathetic as I listen to her story, but I also know what kinds of people developed INFP's can become. I envision her future. Potentially she may be a writer, a psychologist, an artist, a person interested in children's education; or she may be a dancer, an interior designer, an actress. These are fields where imaginative people, such as she is, can be successful, fields that require reflective, inquisitive, empathetic, loyal, idealistic people who are more interested in possibilities than in practicalities. I personally value such people highly, so it is easy for me to love and accept them and to reflect their future back to them.

The female analyst generally receives an idealization projection from these women. She is seen as someone powerful, unique, and admirable. This is tempting to enjoy, of course, but not to be basked in for long. The unremitting depression of the daughter leaves the analyst soon feeling that she is not very powerful at all. As long as the analysand loses her power in projection, she will remain helpless and depressed, and the analyst will be powerless, too. This splitting of power and helplessness effects no positive change for the analysand. As she procrastinates about acting on her understanding of the issues, her passivity and ambivalence toward the analyst and toward life become clear. Her unwillingness to renounce unrealistic dreams and to settle for reality, her "phobia" about commitment, her passive-aggressive behavior, finally produce negative countertransference feelings in the analyst. These feelings have narcissistic roots, of course, inasmuch as the analyst identifies with the healer or with the positive mother complex and expects all analysands to get better and to grow. Of course, this is the complementary side of the analysand's negative mother complex. The analysand's sense of being rejected by the analyst and her unfulfilled wish to be special and unique show up in dreams where, typically, the analyst has too many children or patients, or has a lover, or is eating lunch while the patient is there.

Now the analyst faces the task of shaping this daughter-girl toward social acceptability and pointing her away from her total self-preoccupation. I use the idealizing transference in the same way good-enough mothers do, to socialize their children. Building on a nascent ego, this woman is guided away from excessive rumination. If she does not perform and relate to the world, the consequence is my displeasure. Since my displeasure reconstellates early experiences of separation anxiety, we work through these feelings to gain greater willingness to take risks.

After the analysand has introjected the loved child as reflected in the attitude and gaze of the loving "mother," she can move away from absorption in her inner world toward relationship. She has internalized the necessary conditions for self-esteem by being accepted and loved in an important relationship with an idealized mother figure. When the second step begins, I begin to place qualifiers on love and acceptance: She must now earn them by creating, deciding, producing, and relating. Here the "fathering" begins.

As the analyst moves from the mother to the father role and begins to use the rapport established earlier to elicit certain behaviors from the analysand, resistance occurs. A gamelike quality becomes apparent, with the analysand expecting to be fed, while passive-aggressively refusing to incorporate the food for growth. The longer one stays in the Demeter nurturing role, the more one feels this stubborn resistance and the passive-aggressive qualities that undergird this originally sweet, compliant, good little girl who was trying to please and wanted a mother to love her. A convoluted process occurs which is similar to what the anorexic does with food. The purpose of this craving for love and encouragement is to achieve a state of fusion with the mother-analyst, with whom the analysand identifies. By such an identification, she gains a sense of self-esteem, power, and achievement. But to maintain these, she must become the controller, the withholder, and the rejector, the one who has absolute control over what nourishment is dispensed and eaten. Similar control is applied to her husband, to avoid household duties, financial responsibilities, and his desire for sexual relations.

If the analyst gets caught in an archetypal Demeter role, she will soon experience rejection in such remarks as: "I don't think therapy works"; "I don't know where we're going"; "I don't understand what this is supposed to be doing"; "What are the goals that we are supposed to be having for the next period of time?"; "I don't understand what dreams have to do with any of this." When such negative feelings and doubts about the mother's food erupt, the analyst can easily feel angry. Why is the analysand not getting better? In the inflated archetypal mother identification, one narcissistically requires the analysand-daughter to grow up into an "ideal daughter."

After the analysand has rejected therapy in this manner, she feels guilty and afraid of the analyst's understandable discouragement, frustration, and anger. The analysand sees herself as having ruined the mother who was feeding her. The refusal to take food and to begin to gain competency, to "grow up," is a resistance to becoming a woman and having to accept responsibility.

The struggle to be autonomous by resisting feeding is, in a sense, healthy because it is rebellion against passivity and helplessness. Many young women rebel against the roles of mother and housewife, feeling these do not provide individual identity. In the two-year-old's rebellion, which says "You can't control me, I'll control me," an identity is forming and with it a sense of power to shape others and to control life. Such a woman simply will not be forced into anything. If she is married and has children, she will resist doing housework, keeping the checkbook, and having sexual relations with her husband. These are her passive-aggressive ways of claiming autonomy. The roles of mother and wife, which reinforce her fear of being passive and helpless, fail to provide a good enough identity. Since our culture affords so little status and power to the roles of housewife and mother, her fears are not groundless.

This negative belief system and behavioral pattern need to be lived through and made conscious, so the analysand can choose whether to continue the pattern or not. Otherwise, there is no alternative but regression into an even more infantile place of expecting to be fed or into fantasies of self-annihilation. Here there seems to be no good alternative to either being the infant and pleasing or being the rebel and resisting. The rebellious feelings of anger and the need for power and control, then, are early beginnings of the manifestation of the masculine energies which lead to animus development. Authority, control, competitiveness, assertiveness, instrumentality, and the possession of agentic effectiveness are animus prerogatives. So this negative phase is a forerunner of animus development. By going through it, a woman develops the capacity for independent thought, and this allows her to look at facts, to think logically, and to make her own judgments and decisions based on experience. She learns to express herself in the world and to act.

Without first experiencing the more primitive satisfaction of the desire to please the mother, a woman can fall into a primal death fear and possible regression to deeply unconscious and irrational thought. By reexperiencing this fear in therapy, a woman will be able to leave the underworld realm of Hades. The adolescent daughter returns to her mother, ready now to try new behaviors and be active in the world.

I would like to elaborate on how typology relates to animus development. This earliest stage of animus development ("rape of Kore") seems, from my observation of 30 or more such women over the last several years, to coincide with the INFP type. Of course, it is not completely restricted to one type. Some validation of this clinical observation can be found in an article by Padgett et al. (1982) in *Research in Psychological Type*. These researchers found that some types are more androgynous, while others are prone to assuming sexually stereotyped characteristics. The findings are different for each sex, but the thinking–feeling dimension appears to be critically important for androgyny.

Sex role identification has been receiving a great deal of attention in psychological research as well as in the popular press, with masculinity and femininity no longer seen as mutually exclusive dimensions of personality or behavior. Even introductory psychology textbooks now include discussions of androgyny as an important component of individual personality differences. Comparisons between androgynous and sex-typed persons have been made in relation to expressive versus instrumental behavior, to levels of self-esteem, of independence, and of general adjustment. Androgyny represents the ability to act a wide range of behaviors, not limited by cultural norms or sex role stereotypes. This flexibility is reflected in a great many personality characteristics that differentiate androgynous from sex-typed persons. Examining these differences in terms of the four personality dimensions of the Myers-Briggs Type Indicator, there is strong evidence that the thinking–feeling dimension measures a characteristic associated with androgyny as measured by Sandra Bem's (1974) BEM Sex Role Indicator. Although the majority of androgynous and sex-typed women describe themselves as feeling types, a significantly greater number of androgynous women were categorized on the Myers-Briggs Type Indicator as thinking types, or at least seemed to be able to think and feel as required by the situation.

The personality I am describing as the INFP at the first stage of animus development is, of course, multiply determined. In addition to the factors discussed above, there is probably a biological component. William Sheldon (1940) describes ectomorphic endomorphs as characterized by compassionate empathy, selfless relinquishment, Christian renunciation, while endormorphic ectomorphs are noted for their disinterestedness and detachment. So body type fits the picture I am describing. This type, the ectomorphic endomorph, describes herself as being in a chronic state of fatigue, the least effort bringing about a need to rest. Ordinary routine exhausts her, and she hesitates trying any new task that may tax her. A sense of anxiety, weakness, being overwhelmed and weighted down is a concomitant of this mother-daughter symbiosis and lack of animus agency.

Such women often have the same body type as their mother and often have learned the same behaviors. The mothers also withdraw, lack self-confidence and organizing skills, and lack a relationship to the world. Often the mother's self is hidden behind compliance and the need to meet the demands and expectations of other people, even while she experiences resistance to fulfilling those very demands and expectations.

The analyst can activate a normal progression toward competency and mastery of the environment by encouraging these women to meet challenges and accept new ventures, by demanding responsibililty and encouraging them to "go it alone" in new activities. In this stage, the analyst enacts a father-teacher role. It is crucial here that the analyst not be the "blank screen" and fail to provide guidance, advice, or direction. This fathering side of the therapeutic relationship is necessary for animus development at this stage. It is crucial that the analyst not respond to this kind of an analysand by regarding her as fragile, prone to illness, or as weak and inferior in any way. The analyst can teach the analysand new skills to extend her personal sphere and to get organized. New actions for gaining satisfactions in life must be taught and required. At this point, "bibliotherapy" is encouraged, since these women need information and skills, so practical books are suggested.

The purpose of therapy is to gain a feeling that life is worth living. This purpose is brought about when the young woman learns to be effective in social groups and begins to feel her authority in creative work, and also when she feels she matters in relationship to others. As the analysand's vocabulary for meaning and potential for self-expression increases, she has a clearer picture of who she is, who others are, what life is about, and what is required of her. The development of the richness of her personality can occur from this new center of identity. Therapy in this sense becomes education, with the therapist urging and admonishing her so that she experiences herself differently and is freed from her past sense of worthlessness. If the therapist can mother effectively, the young woman can develop sufficient feminine ego strength. If the analyst can father and teach effectively, she gains competency and is freed from her helpless, masochistic, negativistic, and hopeless self-identification.

In the course of therapy, animus figures slowly change from the destructive, abusive male figures to more helpful, active, and discriminating ones. The threatening dream figures become men of planned action who use initiative and get closure on their plans.

One goal of therapy is to reexperience early control issues, which are the first feeble attempts at autonomy, and to redirect these into more productive areas for growth. The analyst's role is to help the patient develop sufficient ego strength for living an adult life, to help her take steps toward becoming competent in the pursuits of her life, to encourage her to take the next necessary steps, and to discourage her passive-aggressive behavior by confronting it directly. The goal is to assist this woman to change her feelings of self-worth. She has developed a basic attitude that she is flawed, weak, and stupid and that all power to validate her is "out there." The new assumption is that she is capable of being loved and valued, not necessarily as an equal, but as a valued daughter or co-worker, and that she has power within herself.

Negative transference and anger at the analyst can occur when the analysand wants to remain stuck in the position of only receiving nurturance and not giving anything in return. She refuses to give the analyst the gratification of knowing she has helped; she continually needs to discourage the analyst with "Your milk is sour" or "There is not enough of it" messages. She needs the confidence that her own love/"milk" is good in order to enjoy giving. Such young women need to learn to give to others, to their family, to the people they meet, to their husbands, to their analysts.

Such simple things as learning to remember people's names was an early task that an anorexic girl of this typology whom I treated had to learn. She would go in and out of work and social situations never bothering to remember people's names. For months she didn't remember my secretary's name. Poor interpersonal skills of this sort naturally reinforce isolation and communicate aloofness. Small battles like this are selected to prove that she is autonomous. She needs confrontation by the fathering analyst, who will tell her that there are more useful things she can control. The development of initiative is crucial. To get a woman at this stage to envision or to imagine something she could realistically be, or would like to be, working toward, is a large task. Dreams are grandiose and far from her actual abilities. Learning to take small steps toward a chosen goal, however, whether it is going back to college, taking courses in pottery, persisting in dance classes, or merchandising her art, is crucial. The fathering aspect of the analyst offers her guidance for bridging into the world.

Encouragement to join other people, to learn that she has something to give and is not socially inferior, to realize that she can be herself and yet also share herself with other people and handle their critiques without undue sensitivity, can be reinforced in group therapy. In addition to individual analysis, I encourage such young women to join a group where communication patterns can be made conscious and new ones learned. Typically such a woman denies herself, lets others choose for her, remains quiet, feels hurt and anxious in the group. The group members feel guilty that they cannot help her and angry that she does not share herself. She remains passive, demure, tearful, withholding, and isolated. The group helps her see, by their feelings of anger and guilt, how she has the power in this position, and how she reaches her goal at the expense of others, how she excludes the help group members would like to give her in the same way she excludes the nurturing of the analyst. It becomes clearer that she locks other people into a lose–win situation. In her apparently powerless position with regard to the group members or the analyst, she is in fact the more powerful.

In group therapy, the goal for such a person is to learn to be assertive, to confront others, to reveal who she is, to ask for what she wants, to compromise if what she wants cannot be given, and to choose for herself. Then she and the other members can feel mutual respect and shared power, with the willingness to compromise that builds relationship. These attitudes translated into the world make for related, effective living. In the group, she learns social skills for getting power in the world (i.e., to "father" herself).

As all women have, these women have experienced psychological rape by the "masculine" in our culture. Healing comes from mourning and recognizing this rape. The empathy of sisterhood in analysis comes about through recognizing the sadness and pain of the wounding experiences that girls and women suffer as they grow up in our culture where "father knows best." Social and political power inheres in being male. Repeated psychic rapes occur as women enter male-run institutions in this culture, where little girls are sexually abused and women actually raped. The rage that under-lies this woman's depressive position can be faced only if other women understand and support. At this point, therefore, the transference/countertransference must take on a more sisterlike quality and reflect the support of the sisterhood, rather than the nurturing of a loving Demeter-mother or the demands for performance of a Zeus-father and teacher. The empathy of the sisterhood is not regressive, however. It requires that each sister perform in an adult manner, while offering empathy, laughter, and support. If the analyst has not worked through her own rage at her "rape" at varying times in her development, analyst and analysand can regress to a primal rage at men, which is sometimes seen in certain kinds of lesbian relationships or in certain angry, "stuck" feminists.

In addition to a sister transference/countertransference, a colleague and peer transference/countertransference occurs, in which collaboration with an analysand often takes place. I encourage joining of other support groups, so that the support system of sisterhood generalizes to a wider range of women.

In summary, then, the first stage of animus development in therapy requires that a woman be allowed to feel dependent on a strong figure who reflects and nurtures her (mother). Next, she needs to be encouraged to feel that she can strengthen herself, to control herself, and to rely on herself, which leads to confidence that she can have an impact on others (the father/teacher phase). She becomes powerful because she finds she can control herself and affect others. A third transference/countertransference stage occurs as she feels the empathy of a "sister" for the denigration and rape of the feminine that has fostered our mutual powerlessness. At a much later stage, after higher levels of animus development have been reached, the goal of therapy becomes recognizing herself as an instrument of a higher authority to which she can subordinate herself for a nonegoistic goal.

The final stage moves beyond dichotomies of black and white, male and female, good and evil, to a position where one can see many facets of an issue simultaneously and recognize a pattern of interrelatedness. Here paradox is understood and accepted, as one desires to conserve life and to take part in it. When a woman has integrated her life experience to where she can fully express her feminine being, she has full identity and is generative to both men and women. Having compassion for people, a sense of humor, and humility are the marks of this stage (cf. Wiedemann 1982). Some women have reached this highest level, and it is an ideal that women in general are growing toward, as we struggle through the earlier stages of animus development, moving stage by stage toward the integrated woman whose sense of validity and authority comes from an internal partnership of compassion and strength, affiliation and competency. The *coniunctio* of the feminine and masculine in her personality leads back to the community where she gives of herself with loyalty and faith.

References

Bem, S. 1974. Measurement of psychological androgeny. *Journal of Consulting and Clinical Psychology* 42:155–62.

Briggs, K. C., and Myers, I. B. 1979. *Manual: The Myers-Briggs type indicator.* Palo Alto, Calif.: Consulting Psychologists Press.

Eisendrath-Young, P., and Wiedemann, F. L. 1984. Female authority. Manuscript submitted for publication.

Hathaway, S. R., and McKinley, J. C. 1966. *Minnesota multiphasic personality inventory,* rev. ed. New York: Psychological Corporation.

Kersey, D., and Bates, M. 1978. *Please understand me.* Del Mar, Calif.: Prometheus Nemesis Books.

Myers, I. B., and Myers, P. B. 1980. *Gifts differing.* Palo Alto, Calif.: Consulting Psychologists Press.

Neumann, E. 1959. *The psychological stages of feminine development.* Dallas: Spring Publications.

Padgett, H. V.; Cook, D.; Nunley, M.; and Carskadon, T. 1982. Psychological type, androgeny and sex-typed roles. *Research in Psychological Type* 5:69–77.

Sheldon, W. 1940. *Varieties of human physique.* New York: Harper.

Strong, E. K., and Campbell, D. P. 1976. *Strong-Campbell interest inventory,* rev. ed. Palo Alto, Calif.: Stanford University Press.

Ulanov, A. 1979. Fatness and the female. *Psychological Perspectives* 10/1:21.

Wiedemann, F. 1982. The masculine and feminine cooperating and the evolution of human consciousness. Unpublished paper presented at a meeting of the Inter-Regional Society of Jungian Analysts, Galveston, Texas.

Woodman, M. 1980. *The owl was a baker's daughter: Obesity, anorexia nervosa, and the repressed feminine.* Toronto: Inner City Books.

_____. *Addiction to perfection: The still unravished bride.* Toronto: Inner City Books.

Chiron's policy on capitalizing the term "Self"

Jung's understanding of the Self is significantly different from how
this term is often used in other contemporary psychoanalytic literature. The
difference hinges primarily on the understanding of archetypes: The
Jungian conceptualization of the Self sees it as rooted in the transpersonal
dimension. Hence the frequent capitalization of this term. Since the
clinical experience of the Self often takes place within the sphere of ego-
consciousness, however, it can be more mystifying than edifying always
to stress the archetypal level in the literature. Consequently the editors of
Chiron have chosen to allow authors to exercise an option on the
question of capitalization. They may choose to capitalize Self and thereby
to emphasize its transpersonal, archetypal base; or, they may choose to
employ the lower case, signifying by this that they are discussing
issues that have to do principally with ego-identity and the personal
appropriation of this central factor in psychic life, which may be less
precisely articulated by reference to the archetypal substratum.